The Black Seasons

Michał Głowiński

THE BLACK SEASONS

MICHAŁ GŁOWIŃSKI

Translated from the Polish by Marci Shore
Foreword by Jan T. Gross

NORTHWESTERN UNIVERSITY PRESS

Evanston, Illinois

Northwestern University Press
Evanston, Illinois 60208-4170

Printed in the United States of America

1 0 9 8 7 6 5 4 3 2 1

ISBN 0-8101-1958-7 (cloth)
ISBN 0-8101-1959-5 (paper)

Library of Congress Cataloging-in-Publication Data

Michał Głowiński.
[Czarne sezony. English]
The black seasons / Michał Głowiński ; translated from the Polish by
Marci Shore ; foreword by Jan T. Gross.
p. cm. — (Jewish lives)
ISBN 0-8101-1958-7 (cloth : alk. paper) —
ISBN 0-8101-1959-5 (pbk. : alk. paper)
1. Głowiński, Michał—Childhood and youth. 2. Literary historians—
Poland—Biography. 3. Critics—Poland—Biography. 4. Jews—Poland—
Biography. 5. Holocaust, Jewish (1939–1945)—Poland—Personal narra-
tives. I. Shore, Marci. II. Title. III. Series.
PG7011.G58A3 2005
891.8509—dc22

2005004289

⊚ The paper used in this publication meets the minimum requirements of the
American National Standard for Information Sciences—
Permanence of Paper for Printed Library Materials,
ANSI Z39.48-1992.

To the memory of my parents,
Felicja Głowińska, née Rozenowicz,
and Henryk Głowiński

❖

Contents

✿

Foreword

I feel truly privileged introducing *The Black Seasons* to the English-speaking audience. The author of this slender volume, Michał Głowiński, is a public intellectual of great distinction in his native Poland, and the book itself, I am convinced, is destined to enter the canon of Holocaust literature right beside the works of Primo Levi and Tadeusz Borowski.

Głowiński is a professor of literature and a literary critic who established his reputation with theoretical studies of the novel. Three books published in quick succession—*Porządek, chaos i znaczenie* (*Order, Chaos and Meaning,* 1968), *Powieść młodopolska* (*The Novel of Young Poland,* 1969), and *Gry powieściowe* (*Novelistic Games,* 1973)—were hailed for their brilliant and innovative structural approach to the genre. Their author occupies a chair of literary theory at the prestigious Institute of Literary Studies in Warsaw and his seminars are attended by a cohort of bright students, several of whom are already established as the most promising academics of the next generation.

Fortunately for a wider audience of his contemporaries, Głowiński's talent and intellectual curiosity extend far beyond the confines of the history and theory of literature. In addition to being a productive and original scholar, he also has proven to be a brilliant observer of the surrounding reality and an immensely talented writer. True to his professional vocation of a philologist, Głowiński kept detailed notes since the mid-1960s documenting the language of propaganda and public speech spewed by the official media of Communist Poland. Albeit produced in very different circumstances, Głowiński's endeavor may be likened to that of Victor Klemperer, who made a detailed study of the corrupting influence that Nazi speech had on the German language—*Language of the Third Reich* (LTI, Lingua Tertii Imperii)—while keeping a magisterial diary, *I Will Bear Witness,* which made him famous. After the demise of the Communist regime in Poland, Głowiński published his notes and commentary on the language of propaganda in four books documenting and deconstructing the newspeak of mature "real socialism."

In the last decade, he finally turned to yet another literary genre and published several volumes of autobiographical prose. He writes delicately crafted, brief vignettes blending a description of some elusive episode, such as a moment he remembers from childhood, with reflection on the meaning he reads into it from the perspective of knowledge and experience he has since acquired. When *Czarne sezony* came out in Poland in 1998, the book was immediately recognized as a masterpiece and won a nomination for the most prestigious Polish literary prize, Nike. We are indebted to Marci Shore for a brilliant translation of this subtle and deeply moving volume into English.

JAN T. GROSS

PRINCETON UNIVERSITY

✤

Translator's Preface

These extraordinary memoirs of a childhood in the Warsaw
Ghetto were written by a literary theorist fifty years after World
War II. The book is a collage of two voices—that of a young
child and that of his adult self—creating temporal juxtapositions as well as juxtapositions in subject position. Both of Michał
Głowiński's voices are very human and very personal ones, from
which self-righteousness, moralizing, and ideological analysis
are absent. Concerned with authenticity above all else, he writes
with no attempt to fictionalize or aestheticize. Yet his lyrical
prose at once retains a gentle quality and reflects the author's
sensitivity to the deeply subjective nature of memory.

The Black Seasons is structured in imagistic episodes, and the
author pointedly declines to fill in the gaps or to reconstruct
from other sources moments missing from his own memory. The
Polish literary critic Jacek Leociak writes in his review of *The
Black Seasons* that the text presents before us "an archipelago of
memory" and that "the world which emerges on the pages of this
book is not only condemned to fragmentariness, but also on
more than one occasion seems to be composed of coincidental,
unimportant elements. *The Black Seasons* is as much about what
is described as about that which lies beyond the possibility of
description, beyond the space of memory, beyond the border
of consciousness." In this way the structure is self-consciously fragmented, yet paradoxically—or, perhaps, for this reason—the
text taken as a whole is remarkably fluid.

This fluidity comes into being in its original language in part
through uncommonly long, spilling sentences, creating a stream-
of-consciousness effect as well as conjuring a sense of the unstruc-

tured and often overwhelming nature of memory. These lengthy, flowing sentences have often (although not always) been among the "necessary losses" of translation. I have tried to balance the impulse toward stylistic preservation with the exigencies of English prose. Polish, like Latin, is an inflected language, meaning that the function of a noun in a sentence is determined by its case ending as opposed to its position. The result of this inflection is a tremendous increase in flexibility in word order and a resulting ability to sustain a succession of clauses in a way that English cannot do without great strain.

One further structural disparity between Polish and English in particular bears mentioning. Polish, like other Slavic languages, makes heavy use of the passive voice through impersonal verb forms, reflexive constructions, and subjectless sentences. The linguistic distinction could be understood to reflect more broadly an existential one: in Slavic languages, the self often becomes, rather than the subject of the sentence, the indirect object, the recipient of fate. In English the passive voice often seems all too obviously to obscure—or conceal—agency. In Slavic languages agency is perhaps less concealed than it is simply too ethereal to be grasped. In the hopes of evoking a sense of the original Polish, I have tried to preserve the impersonal voice when possible; when the syntax was just too awkward for English, I transposed the voice into an active one.

In connection with this structural issue is one concerning vocabulary. A certain Polish word, *zginąć,* appears with particular frequency in Głowiński's text—as it does more generally in connection with World War II and the Holocaust. *Zginąć* embraces a cluster of English meanings: to die, to die violently in the sense of suddenly, to be killed, to perish, to disappear, to vanish, to become not-there-anymore. Again, agency may or may not be present and is somewhat ethereal, hovering in that liminal space between life and death, presence and absence. The word comprises a certain motif in the original text that had to be lost in translation, as it was impossible to translate in all instances with a single English word.

The themes of these memoirs are as nuanced and multivalent as the stories that evoke them. While Głowiński makes no pronouncements on the angst-laden issue of Polish–Jewish relations, the whole book is, in a sense, about just that. The reader meets through the eyes of the child-narrator Poles who made very different, very complicated choices during the war, and so experiences a story more about individuals and individual choices than about nations and national character. *The Black Seasons* serves as well as an implicit deconstruction of all deterministic narratives of that time. Głowiński's story is one of radical contingency, in which his own survival was never assured and was rather always dependent upon precariously contingent events. This is a story of how it was he survived, told with an acute awareness that at any moment things might have been otherwise. In the final pages the author brings the reader into the present and reflects on those traces of wartime childhood experiences that have lingered within him.

Together with the war, memory itself comprises a central theme of the book. The text is framed by the motif of the liminal space between memory and forgetting—a border "always already" in flux, a border whose location may be arbitrary and even capricious. Głowiński continually, as if compulsively, draws the reader's attention to what he remembers versus what he has forgotten, what he remembers barely and vaguely as opposed to well and clearly, what others might have remembered differently had they lived, what is certain, almost certain, perhaps certain or perhaps not at all certain, what will forever remain unknown.

Głowiński himself is a literary theorist, and his writing here is subtly yet distinctly informed by postmodern critiques of historical narrative. His commitment is to authenticity over coherence, and he writes with acute self-consciousness of the limitations of memory and the problems of narrative. Głowiński, himself a writer, hesitated for fifty years before writing about himself and what happened to him during the years of the Holocaust. While he makes no mention of Theodor Adorno, Adorno's warning—that artistic representation of the Holocaust is barbarism, and there can be no poetry after Auschwitz—lurks as a subtext throughout. Yet at once an aesthetic dimension to Głowiński's prose remains, in truth as in fiction, inherent in the very language, the title itself an intertextual allusion to the refrain of fellow survivor Paul Celan's haunting *Todesfuge:* "black milk of daybreak we drink you at night."

I remain enormously grateful to the following people: Bill Johnston, Anna Frajlich, Jan T. Gross, Christopher Howard, Mateusz Kosz, Sławomir Kędzierski, Jacek Leociak, Madeline Levine, Rafael Minc, Olimpia Nowicka, Piotr Sommer, and John Waddell at various points answered specific linguistic questions on topics ranging from mildew stains to priestly garments. Amelia Glaser, Gail Glickman, Agata Jagiełło, Meredeth Rouse, Daniel Shore, Timothy Snyder, and Stephanie Steiker all read and commented at length on drafts or various parts thereof. I am indebted as well to the author, who spent one long afternoon with me in Warsaw, helping me to decipher some of the more cryptic references in his rich text, and who has been warm and supportive throughout.

The Black Seasons

❖

Author's Note

When I first began to set down these stories in writing, I did not anticipate their comprising a book. Each of them is a relation of an experience, emerging from flashes of memory, neither embracing the entirety of events nor encompassing all of my life and the history of how I survived during those years. These stories are rather of a different character, and I was unconcerned with their unity. I was unable to sketch a continuous record—the gaps in my memory revealed themselves to be too great—and I felt that filling these gaps with fiction, conjectures, and even information drawn from other sources available in various forms would be highly inappropriate and a departure from my intent here. Flashes of memory possess their own rules; they dissolve concerns about consistency and justify fragmentariness—indeed, they assume this from the outset. And they give impetus to heterogeneity. I write of what I have remembered, and when I am not certain of something, I say so openly. Readers should not wonder when from time to time they encounter the phrase "I don't know." These stories are composed solely of what I experienced and what I have remembered. In confining myself to what I myself went through, in writing only of my own fate and at times of those who influenced it, I would like to believe that I have avoided repeating what has already been said, what is already known, or what is generally accessible knowledge—and yet I hope that in so doing, I am not depriving these stories of certain, more transcendent, meanings.

✿

Fragments from the Ghetto

A Word

I remember when I heard it for the first time. It was at the very beginning of the war, right after the defeat. The word drifted into my ears as people around me deliberated: will they lock us in the ghetto or not? I didn't know what this word meant, yet I realized it was connected with moving. I sensed that it was something adults spoke of with fear, but to me, it seemed that moving would be an interesting adventure. And in the end I envisioned this mysterious and incomprehensible ghetto as a huge, many-storied carriage riding through the streets of the city, pulled by some umpteen horses. Into such a carriage they would put us, and we would live there; on the whole it would turn out to be something quite exciting and entertaining. I imagined that in this carriage there would be all kinds of staircases, so that one could run freely from one floor to the next, and many windows as well, so that nothing would stand in the way of looking out over the unknown world. In my imagination, I conjured up this fantastical carriage on the model of a hearse—the black carriage of death—such as could be seen from time to time in our city. Quickly, though, I would be forced to part with these child-like phantasmagoria. We did in fact move, but it did not turn out to be a fascinating adventure. And in the very near future direct experience would instruct me in the precise meaning of this

5

word. Little time had passed before I no longer entertained any doubts as to its implications, even though such a short time before, it had sounded so mysterious, so exotic, so intriguing.

Color

To this day I still don't understand that space encircled by walls. I'm not able to grasp it, to capture it, I'm not able to discern the principles by which it was organized. That space remains for me a chaos, impossible to comprehend. And this is so not only when I reminisce, when I try to remember how I observed it at the time, when I was shut inside it. This is also true today when I look at a map of what was once the old Jewish quarter, a place that would so quickly reveal itself to be the site of collective death. That space remains for me a tangle of streets connected in a way I'm unable to penetrate. I'm unable to place where we lived, I'm unable to point to what felt close and what far away. I know now that spatial images had no objective dimension, for behind the walls—as in any prison or camp, or more generally, in any place that can be described as a penal colony—peculiar spatial relations come into being. In my memory, that tangle of streets was never empty for a moment. I was not out, naturally, after the curfew, nor during those times when, by the nature of the situation, everything was desolate. I saw those streets during the day and was one of the crowd, a dense crowd that was barely possible to squeeze through.

The ghetto remains in my memory as a place without a shape, deprived of any ordering principle, a space enclosed by walls from which all sense has been taken, just as the sense of life was taken from those pressed within it. Yet I remember its color, unique and inimitable, the sort of color that might signify every collective misfortune: a gray-brown-black, the only one of its kind, devoid of any brighter color or distinguishing accent. Before my eyes remains this monochromatism of the ghetto, perhaps best described by the word "discoloredness." For everything

was just that—discolored—regardless of what its original color
had been and irrespective of the weather. Even the most inten-
sive rays of sunlight would not brighten or even vaguely tint this
discoloredness. But did the sun ever shine in the ghetto? Can the
sun appear in a place without an inch of green?

In my memories, the color of the ghetto is the color of the paper that covered the corpses lying in the street before they were
taken away. The corpses belonged to the permanent landscape,
as the street was a place of death: not only sudden and unexpected death, but also slow death—from hunger, from disease,
from every other possible cause. The season of great dying lasted
in the ghetto without interruption. These bodies covered with
sheets of paper never failed to make an intense impression on me,
and that paper itself became for me one of death's embodiments,
one of its symbols. I'm unable to describe its distinctive color;
afterward, I never again saw such paper, yet I think that the description "discolored" would be closest, most fitting. Precisely
that color without color—neither white nor ash nor even gray—
defines the colorscape of the ghetto and imparts its tone. And
that permanent discoloredness inscribed itself in my mind. I was
much astonished when I suddenly encountered it—made real
and tangible—once again. I was at the cinema, watching Andrzej Wajda's black-and-white film about Janusz Korczak. This
was not an ordinary black-and-whiteness—and not only because
the director made use of black and white at a time when color
dominated the screen. It was not ordinary because it came to signify the color of the ghetto, that grayness with no boundaries,
no differentiation. Watching the film, I could not believe my
eyes. I was seeing that discolored color—in essence, the antith-
esis of color—in the very form in which it had imprinted itself
in my memory decades earlier. And if only for capturing this col-
orless color of the ghetto, I am grateful to Andrzej Wajda for that
unusual and important film, which some fanatics have attacked
for reasons difficult to fathom.

Scenes from the Street

I'm reflecting on what has stayed in my memory from the streets of the ghetto, apart from a generalized picture in which the streets form a labyrinthine web, into which stumbles not a lone wanderer, but a humiliated crowd, systematically deprived of all rights, not yet fully aware that the greatest right—that of life— would be taken from it as well. Some fragments have also remained, details having only vague significance vis-à-vis general knowledge, but which for me are important as traces, pressed deeply in my consciousness, of those places and of those times.

I don't know why this scene in particular became fixed in my memory so forcefully, as there was nothing to distinguish it as something that would fascinate a small child. I was walking with someone from my family—not my mother this time—along one of the overcrowded streets when suddenly on the street I saw a rickshaw or a droshky. (But were there droshkies in the ghetto? It was a world deprived of natural things, I don't remember that I ever saw a horse there.) In it rode a festively dressed young couple, obviously returning from their wedding. The newlyweds gave the impression of being happy, the young man held his companion by the hand. It was certainly for two reasons that I remembered that snapshot, in itself of no larger significance. First, it seemed as though displaced from another world, transcending those things that constructed the reality in which I was living. Possibly I saw it as a scene extracted from a fairy tale. There was, though, still another reason. The newlyweds were not riding away from their wedding in a golden carriage, yet they drew the attention of passersby who made no attempt to conceal their distaste: a honeymoon, even if only from one ghetto street to another, was apparently not suited to this reality, it seemed inappropriate. I remember that a boy shouted to the young man: "That one, hold onto her, or she'll get away." Maybe I'm conflating that scene with another, from another day and another place—I can't exclude that possibility—but it seems to me that just then I saw the Germans filming this very street in the ghetto. Perhaps the image of the young couple was meant to attest to the propaganda that calm prevailed in the Warsaw Ghetto, that life proceeded normally.

Another fragment from these streets that has lingered in my mind has an entirely different character, even if only because it concerned not a singular and atypical occurrence, but rather a scene that repeated itself with great regularity—perhaps to say every day would not be an exaggeration. As I walked to the lessons taught by Panna Julia and Pani Bronisława, I would pass on my way there—which after all was not very far—an emaciated man, no longer young, playing the violin. He always played the same tune, which I learned from one of the adults was a fragment of Mendelssohn's Violin Concerto. It was said that before the war the violinist had been a member of the Warsaw Philharmonic Orchestra, and only the extreme poverty of the ghetto had forced him onto the streets. I can still see his figure before my eyes. There was so little of him that he faded away into his wide gray overcoat, which undoubtedly had fit him during better prewar times, but which now hung on him as if made for three such men as him. He played all the time, regardless of the weather, wearing a hat, which like the coat seemed much too large for him, his face was lost in the shadow of the wide brim. Everything associated with him—apart from the melody that came from his violin—was connected to grayness, and so existed in harmony with the general color scheme of the ghetto. I don't know if people threw offerings to him; I can't imagine how he could have collected them, since his instrument occupied both his hands. He must have succeeded in collecting something, given that he played every day, but these would have been sums insufficient to provide for even the most basic needs. Destitution and hunger were ever more visible in his appearance. A skeleton, clothed in an overcoat, playing the violin.

Viewings of Death

I've mentioned already the corpses covered with paper lying on the street. That scene was my first meeting with death, and it sank into my imagination. Still, this was an anonymous, impersonal death, as I didn't know any of those who had ended their span of years on the sidewalks of the ghetto. Yet in the season of great dying, even a child's experience of death could not be limited to this type of random encounter; death was encroaching from all sides and would come to assume a more personal form. Very quickly I grasped the essence of the matter: a person was— and suddenly is no more. My becoming conscious of this fact was yoked with terror; it was a consciousness that evoked a fear difficult to overcome. It seems to me today, so many years later, that I never managed to get used to it, even in the conditions of the ghetto where contact with dying belonged to the sphere of everyday occurrences, commonplace and banal.

My first experience of death, beyond the sight of corpses lying on the street, was not connected with the departure of someone close to me or even of someone I knew well. Rather it was connected with someone whom I had seen only a few times; I didn't even know (and don't know to this day) his name. He was a tall, very thin man, slightly hunchbacked, whose movements— it seemed to me—were as if mechanical. In general he gave the impression of one who had been artificially put together from different parts: his head, with oddly protruding cheeks and wire glasses falling down his nose, gave the impression of having been fastened with screws onto the rest of his body. This strange man evoked in me a panicked fright. Perhaps that's why I remember him so vividly, although, of course, I have no assurance that the picture which has lasted in my memory corresponds to the actual person. (Many years later I imagined several characters from Hoffmann's fantastical tales in just such a way.) I saw him from time to time when I went to Pani Anna for lessons; he lived in the same apartment as she did, and he may have been her cousin. One day when I knocked on the door at the usual time, I was told there would be no lessons today, because the man whose very appearance had so frightened me had just died. Soon it reached me that he had hanged himself in the bathroom the night before. The image of that dead man dangling in the bathroom haunted me for a long time afterward—and I think that it was just then, being no more than seven years old, that I grasped what death was. That man, somewhat resembling a scarecrow, became my emblem of death.

Only once did I witness a killing. It happened later, I think in the time just before the beginning of the *Aktion,* the transports to Treblinka. We were living someplace else then, close to the ghetto wall, in an apartment where the kitchen windows looked out onto the kind of courtyard-well so characteristic of the Warsaw of times past. I heard screams, and I wanted to see what was happening. Several Germans were gathered in a narrow, tight space, and in front of a wall several men stood. The execution began. I don't know who the victim was or what was the immediate provocation. I only saw a shot fired and a person fall. My mother pulled me away from the window; the shots that followed I only heard, resonating oddly inside the courtyard. She didn't want me to be a witness to the successive horrors, although I had already seen more than one; she worried, too, that the Germans would begin firing upward at those who were leaning out of their windows. I don't know how many people died that time; I remember, though, the enormous pool of blood in the courtyard. That scene stayed in my consciousness in the form of a snapshot, a momentary occurrence. My thoughts didn't often return to it, for now the season of great dying had entered its culminating phase, and even for a child it was difficult to revisit earlier events. The dominant place in my consciousness came to be occupied by two words not heard earlier: "Umschlagplatz" and "Treblinka."

The Cellar

The story I will tell now happened already in the final phase when those two words were on the lips of everyone locked behind the walls. The liquidation *Aktion* had only just begun; that day our turn came. We were to be herded off to Umschlagplatz—and delivered directly to the gas chambers. My family and a good number of our neighbors (perhaps all of them?) hid inside one of the cellars, the one located farthest away from the entrance, although certainly not especially well concealed. As far as I can remember, the building caretaker locked the cellar from the outside. I can still see him: he was a young, tall, broad-shouldered man. He himself wasn't yet hiding—he must have judged that the role he served would protect him from the transport—but his wife was probably with us. And, indeed, he was not taken this time.

It's difficult for me today to say very much about our time in hiding, as the details have faded into the mist. It was crowded, and the vault was so low that it was impossible to stand. I already understood well what was going on, what we wanted to escape by hiding in a place not meant for human habitation. Every sound approaching from the outside brought terror. And I, too—understandably—was overcome with fear. I nestled close to my parents, though in such a situation, even they were not a guarantee of safety—I realized that they were threatened by the same thing as I was, as we all were. It was dark, absolute silence was obligatory, no sign of life was permitted to escape from behind those walls.

I remember best this episode: at a certain moment, the silence was radically broken. One of the women hiding with us (perhaps she was the wife of the building caretaker?) was holding in her arms an infant, likely not more than a few months old. The infant began crying convulsively and wouldn't be quieted. The mother rocked her baby and covered its mouth; finally the baby was given a sedative. There were whispers that we would be discovered and killed because of the child. Voices arose that the child had to be suffocated—if not, the baby together with all of us hiding in the cellar would die. A debate began; the young woman would not agree to the murder of her child. It didn't come to that, perhaps because the infant calmed down, or perhaps because the tension was dissipated by a man who said, "That child will be our talisman. It will bring us luck." The rules of memory are strange; of that whole experience, I remember most clearly those words—perhaps because lurking behind them was hope. In fact, shortly thereafter the caretaker appeared and opened the cellar. The team of *szaulisi* and *czubaryki* assisting the Germans had gone. This time we had succeeded in evading the road to Umschlagplatz.

I don't know how much time we spent in the cellar, it was probably several hours. Yet even if I were to know, it would have no greater meaning—such time cannot be measured by the usual dimensions, at moments like this clocks reveal themselves to be instruments of little use. I think this as well because that sojourn in the cellar has remained with me to this day, it didn't come to an end with the opening of the doors—and not only because the danger remained even after the concrete threat had passed. In a world in which the only governor and lawmaker is a crime systematically executed according to a plan imposed from above, threats and danger do not end—their final phase can only come in their fulfillment, their full realization, after which there remains nothing. Of course I wasn't aware of that in the summer of 1942; I wasn't yet eight years old. I think, though, that the majority of the adults knew. And with full certainty those who judged that the principle *contra spem spero* was not applicable here—as in situations of finality, it manifests its uselessness—were aware of how things stood.

It was my first encounter with that kind of confinement. Earlier I had learned what confinement was when we were transferred to the Warsaw Ghetto from the ephemeral ghetto in Pruszków; that trip in a sealed railway car lasted two days, even though just over a dozen kilometers separated my family's town from the capital. Even so, this was something different.

The Road to Umschlagplatz

I remember it only from a certain moment, the moment when we found ourselves in the crowd, pushed and dragged through the streets by the Germans and their Ukrainian and Lithuanian-

Latvian accessories as well as by Jewish policemen. I cannot say how we were taken from our home; that episode has been blocked from my memory, most likely because I was so terrified that my consciousness didn't register what was happening. I'm certain, though, that we were taken from our apartment, not from the cellar. Perhaps my parents conceded that there was no longer any sense in hiding; perhaps they were caught by surprise, not having expected we would be taken on this particular day. I regret not having asked them while they were alive. Perhaps they would have been able to answer my questions—even though they'd hung a curtain of silence over their experiences and revisited them only unwillingly, as if remembering amounted to a renewal of suffering, suffering that was impossible—and impermissible— to forget, but also difficult to speak of.

I remember that they took some kind of baggage: my father, a backpack, and my mother, a purse. They must have packed the most essential things, maybe some food. I don't know if they got those small bags ready at the last moment—or did they have them ready to grab at the moment when it would happen? I don't know if they really believed they would need those things, or if they took them just in case, because one didn't set off on a trip without them, even if one were going directly to the gas chambers. Did they know then that this was where the journey led? Or did they, even if only in some small measure, harbor illusions as well? Of course the question doesn't concern only them. That day most—or maybe all—had brought bags with them, at least a few modest possessions. Yet I don't know whether these bundles were a sign that somewhere in the depths of their consciousness, despite everything, lingered a faith in survival. Of course I don't know what I felt myself at the time—apart from fear and terror. In many situations, especially of this kind, a child has the status of an object. This was truer still since everyone herded off in the march to Umschlagplatz had the status of incapacitated beings. My parents must have taken care that I didn't lose all hope.

I don't remember how the day began, although I think that it must have begun as did other days during the time of liquidation and transports. And about this I do have something to say: we lived right by the wall, and from the window of our room we could see and hear the Aryan Side. And we heard, and saw, the divisions shouting out Nazi songs as they marched in close formation toward the ghetto, the clicking of boots moving closer. There was no doubt as to why those divisions were headed behind the walls. The *Aktion* was fully underway. Undoubtedly this day began similarly as well. Did we know then that on just this day we would find ourselves at Umschlagplatz?

As I've written, I remember that procession only from a certain moment. When we'd neared our destination, a selection was carried out. This was what it was called—and to this day the word "selection" is so powerfully yoked to precisely this experience that I'm unable to use it with any equanimity, even though I'm aware that it can appear in various contexts, in reference to various spheres of reality. The selection consisted of this: from the stream of people, a small group not destined that day for the transport—a small group that was to remain—was sectioned off. When it was our turn, it seemed to me that we had been among those designated to stay. I didn't realize then that the journey would be a final one, but even so I preferred to avoid it. I wanted to go home. I started to jump for joy—for a moment I was happy—and it was only after two or three minutes that I oriented myself to the fact that we hadn't, after all, found ourselves among the chosen, that we were rather in the main group being sent toward Umschlagplatz. Exaltation metamorphosed into despair. Of the whole day I remember this moment most vividly.

When we reached Umschlagplatz, the freight cars were already waiting, the train was preparing to set off. It was crowded. That day the Germans had taken more people than they could transport, and some would have to stay behind. I remember that some people had their names written in capital letters on their backpacks. It was hot, the sun was shining. The season of great dying reached its fullness at the height of summer—this contradicts what I've written about the sun's never shining over the ghetto. Though when the sun did appear, it, too, was cruel and

inhuman, like everything else behind the ghetto walls, it intensified suffering, it brought no hope, but rather scorched even
more those condemned to death. A conversation between my parents has imprinted itself in my memory. My mother suggested
we push our way onto the train about to depart, so as to get this
over with more quickly. Had she oriented herself to the fact that
this was a transport to death? My father was of a different opinion. He judged that we should stay as far away from the railway
tracks as possible, as we might yet succeed in extricating ourselves from Umschlagplatz. As the course of events revealed, it
was he who was right.

Although I was present, I don't know exactly how it happened,
I'm unable to narrate these events with any order. After the train
to Treblinka had departed, Umschlagplatz grew less crowded. A
certain group of people remained—those who, like us, had been
driven from the farthest areas of the ghetto and so had arrived
the latest. People settled temporarily in spots on the ground,
each one, like my parents, likely thinking of how to get out. It
was chance that rescued us. My father met someone he'd known
in his youth, someone whom he hadn't seen in years and who was
now a Jewish policeman. My father asked him to help us escape,
and this man led us somewhere toward the back. He put us in a
dark place, something resembling a packing room or a narrow
corridor where some kind of household goods must have once
been stored. We were to stay there until the German divisions,
having completed their tasks for the day, left the ghetto. And
so it happened. That acquaintance from years past led us out of
Umschlagplatz via a side exit, perhaps through a hole in the
fence.

We survived, my parents and I. In truth, I don't understand
how it happened, I'm unable to grasp the way in which chance
revealed itself to be so favorable to us. I'm astonished. I'm astonished by all of it. I'm astonished that I'm alive. But I live, I
am, I exist . . . and I remember!

The Pastry

It's tremendously difficult for me to begin this story, and not only because it brings the horror to life again, the horror of things one doesn't want to revisit—yet evading this revisiting lies outside the realm of the possible as well. It's difficult most of all because my time in the ghetto constitutes a single block, at least until the moment when the transports began, and thus the moment when what had already seemed most terrible was transformed into something still more terrible, something so extraordinarily evil that there are no more words with which to speak about it. I'm unable to master this block, to introduce differentiations. In particular, I'm largely unable to separate what I remember as a small child in the ghetto from what I later heard and read. And so I realize that in not wanting to repeat what has already been said, I can safely tell only of my own experiences, those belonging to me alone. The story I will now tell fulfills this condition.

It happened at the beginning of our stay in the Warsaw Ghetto, just after we were moved from the short-lived (one wants to say "ephemeral") ghetto in Pruszków. Initially we lived near a wooden bridge connecting the two sides of Chłodna Street; this bridge defined the landscape of the neighborhood and imprinted itself so well in my memory that to this day I can see it before me. In my family, basic needs were met. I hadn't then yet felt hunger. Everything, however, that fell beyond basic needs could only be the object of a child's fantasy and so naturally became an enormous attraction, enticing the imagination. Such was the case when I was promised a pastry as a reward. As a reward, because I was sick. I'd fallen ill with—if I'm not mistaken—a lingering flu with complications of some sort, and perhaps with whooping cough as well. In general I wasn't a child who caused any special problems, but as a patient I was onerous, simply atrocious; I wouldn't allow myself to be touched, I grumbled and squirmed. The pastry was to be a reward for my good behavior as a patient. My fantasies fixated upon it, they sustained me, I couldn't wait until I'd gotten better and would go with my mother to the nearby pastry shop and make that wonderful, long-anticipated purchase. We'd walked by that shop many times, but I'd never been inside. For me, the window in which two or three pastries were usually on display was an unusual, inaccessible, magical world.

At last the long-awaited moment drew near. I chose the pastry that appealed to me most and that (or so I imagined) would taste the best. I didn't eat it there in the shop, though. My mother explained that I should eat it at home, in a peaceful setting, as it should be a full celebration, a kind of ceremony. I still remember what the pastry looked like—on the surface there was a layer of red jelly. The woman working at the shop wrapped it up elegantly, tying the package with a thin, colored string. It was by this string that I held this much-desired object that had been promised to me beginning a week or so earlier. I was happy. I didn't even vaguely anticipate what was about to occur. We'd barely managed to walk several meters away from the shop, when a ragged kid (in the ghetto these children were called *hotsrakhmunes*), definitely a bit older than I but not by very much, ran toward me and tore that immensely precious and long-awaited package from my hand. He had escaped only a few steps when, still running, he began to devour the pastry. It all happened in literally the blink of an eye. Was he so terribly hungry that he couldn't stand to wait even a moment? Or was he afraid that his conquest would be seized from him as well? Over half a century has passed, yet to this day I still see that scene with such clarity, as if it had just occurred yesterday, a week ago at most. I can see that ragged kid—a living skeleton—devouring the pastry as if he wanted to swallow the paper along with it. The event was a shock for me, in a sense my world collapsed. I wasn't yet seven years old and already I had come to see that, along with everyone else, I was living in a terrifying world. Of course I still didn't entirely understand it. Thanks to my parents, who protected me as much as they could, I had yet to experience the worst. I didn't yet know suffering in the form of hunger. I reacted with a convulsive sobbing, which I was entirely unable to overcome. It became more intense, then turned into howling and gnashing of teeth. I think that by then the matter had transcended the ill-fated pastry. I'd seen how terrible the world was, I'd grasped that nothing would any longer happen as I wanted it to, that I was vulnerable to aggression, and that what I wanted for my own and what mattered to me would be taken away. By then I'd already seen various horrible things. I'd seen corpses lying on the ghetto streets covered with a strange paper whose sallow color is difficult to describe, and these affected me. The incident of the pastry, though, was the first cruel lesson imparted to me so directly and so personally.

When I think about it today, the question comes to me: how did my parents try to console me and explain what had happened? I'm certain that my grandfather, who had an owner's mentality and for whom property, regardless of the circumstances, would always be property, unequivocally condemned the assailant. Yet what did my parents say to me? What did I hear from them? Did they tell me: something bad happened, something painful, but you have to understand one thing—that poor, wretched boy was hungry, and you weren't hungry; for you, it was only a matter of a special treat? I admit that today I'd be happy to think that such words were said to me then, but how it was really, I don't know. And I'm never to find out.

❖

Emil

Around this time I was going to Panna Julia and Pani Bronisława for lessons. They were sisters, prewar teachers who,
for a small fee, taught a class of several children. These weren't
my first lessons; earlier my parents had sent me to a little school
run by Pani Anna. At that time we were living in the ghetto's
outskirts, and so had to leave when, at a certain moment, the
Germans eliminated that area from the territory of the ghetto.
Pani Anna as well moved to a different apartment, now too far to
go to for lessons, especially since the streets of the sealed quarter
were becoming more and more dangerous and one never knew
what could happen. The room where Panna Julia and Pani Bronisława resided wasn't far from the tiny room into which we had
moved, which was also on the outskirts of the ghetto, but different outskirts, right by the wall, not visible (or imaginable)
from the Aryan Side. Only a few buildings separated us. I remember, though, the path I had to cross. Lying along it were often the corpses of those who had starved to death, covered with
sheets of gray paper. I remember as well the closeness of the wall,
marking the space where every living thing was condemned
irrevocably to death. There is much that I remember . . . yet I
know there is still more that I don't remember.

I remember the room where our lessons were held: it was oblong, with a large window and three small tables put together
for our arrival so as to create some semblance of a classroom. A

small, provisional kitchen had been installed in one of the corners, and in the other corner Pani Bronisława's husband, Pan
Mieczysław, usually sat. Before the war he had been a journalist
for one of the Polish-language Jewish newspapers, and so in the
ghetto he found himself among those unable to work in their
own professions, without employment, and he had a lot of time.
During our classes he would usually read; sometimes he would
listen, bored, to the lessons conducted by his wife and sister-in-
law. I don't remember what he looked like. I can, though, still
see before me the small and fragile Pani Bronisława, and Panna
Julia as well, who deserves her own description. She was tall and
frighteningly thin, that morbid thinness brought about by disease and malnutrition, so characteristic of people in the ghetto.
In the summer she wore a dark dress with short sleeves, and so
we could see her arms, yellowed and emaciated, nothing but skin
and bones. Her oblong face with its sunken cheeks could seem
frightening, her features had taken on a sharpness they had no
doubt lacked during better times. She was a kind person, although someone could have thought she resembled a witch, or
personified death. As I recall these women, I think of something
else: it's possible I am the only one who remembers them, the
only one who knows that they once lived, worked, taught—and
perished—together with the world of which they were a part.
And mine must be the only memory in which remain my classmates, Panna Julia and Pani Bronisława's pupils. I don't know
their surnames, and I remember only some of their first names.
I see before me Suzi, who was fully grown and a bit older, speaking Polish oddly, because she had been born in Hamburg, and
the Germans had removed her family to the Polish border only
just before the war. I see before me the fair-haired, smiling Mela,
who once with great feeling related an unusual and joyous event
of the previous day: she had eaten broth with noodles for lunch.
I see before me a black-haired girl who collected stamps, now
anonymous, as I'm unable to recall her name. And finally I see
before me Tadzio—although I'm not certain this was his name—
always energetic and unruly, who liked to boast of his father who

was, or so he claimed, a prominent lawyer. He called me giraffe, because it seemed to him I had an amusingly long neck. And I can no longer see anyone else from our class, although there were more of us. In my memory of that murdered world only remnants, fragments, shreds have remained.

There does remain, however, a boy whom I never met in person, although I saw him several times. His name was Emil and he was the living legend of our class. When I joined the group, he was no longer among us, although both teachers remembered him with warmth, affection, and admiration. His classmates remembered him with fondness. He must have been a likeable boy (he wasn't more than nine), as well as brilliant. Emil was spoken of as someone exceptional, unusually talented, surpassing all of us. One child or another would relate how he had met Emil on one of the ghetto streets walking with his mother; someone else would say that he had heard something of Emil's fate. Even in his absence he was still present among us. He was in the ghetto with his mother, but his father, too, was spoken of with admiration and curiosity. An officer in the Polish army, his father was a prisoner in a camp far away—and naturally wasn't able to care for his wife and son. Once during the break between classes (Panna Julia and Pani Bronisława's lessons resembled a school), someone looked out the window and from the second floor saw Emil. Excitement followed: Emil's coming, Emil's coming. They called out: *Emil, come to us!* Emil didn't come, though—he walked on with his mother along one of the overcrowded streets of the ghetto near the wall. His mother had given up sending him to the lessons when she had fallen into such extreme poverty that she was no longer able to set aside the small fee to pay for them. We knew that Panna Julia and Pani Bronisława wanted to waive any fees; they wanted to teach Emil, who was the pearl of the group and everyone's favorite, for free. We knew that they'd asked his mother to consent, that they'd asked many times, even pressured her, but she always refused. Maybe she refused because her pride wouldn't permit her to do otherwise. Maybe she was afraid that her son, the only one excused from paying tuition, would find himself in a humiliating position, that his classmates would remind him of his privileged circumstances. It's possible that it was about something else: perhaps Emil's mother regarded him as being so talented as to make the lessons unnecessary, as he already knew so much and after the war, when he needed to, he would quickly make up for any shortcomings. In this way he became our model and our myth—perhaps precisely because of his absence. That I remember his story so well, after more than half a century, testifies to how much he was spoken of among us.

I don't know what happened to him, and so I don't know if he had the opportunity to fill in the gaps in his education after the war. I would suppose, though, that he wasn't given the chance, that he died as did most of the others. Our summer break began, as in normal schools, in the last days of June—and never came to an end. When 22 July 1942 came, the last phase of the Final Solution commenced. Once the transports from Umschlagplatz began, the continuation of anything was out of the question. I know with complete certainty that Panna Julia and Pani Bronisława, together with Pan Mieczysław, did not survive the war. They died in Treblinka. Yet I don't know the fate of my peers. I know nothing not only of Emil, whom I never met, but also of Suzi, who spoke Polish with a German accent. I know nothing of the smiling Mela, I know nothing of the small girl with black hair and dark, sad eyes who collected stamps (I also collected stamps, and for this reason the detail stuck in my mind). I know nothing of the unruly Tadzio. And I know even less of what happened to those whom I don't remember. I don't know of their fates, yet I can't help but think that they all died, and that what I've written is a collective epitaph. I can't exclude the possibility that I am the only one living, that I am the only one of that class, whose oldest member was less than ten years old, who remembers its existence and is able to say something about it. It's difficult to think of oneself as the only witness and still more difficult to live with that awareness. After all, I can't help but question why I am the one among the living and not the marvelous and exceptional Emil, Suzi with her odd Polish, or the unruly Tadzio. Why? There is no answer to this kind of question. One can only reflect upon whether Emil, for example, would have better, more wisely, more creatively made use of the unusual gift of life—the life of a person who was condemned to extermination while still in his childhood.

❖

My Grandfather's Suicide

I met him only a few times in my life and he left few traces in my memory, unlike my maternal grandfather, whom I knew from my earliest childhood and for a long time, as he survived the war and died only in 1952, when I was already a university student. Yet I've decided to set down some words about the grandfather I knew far less well, because I admire him for a decision made in a moment of extremity.

He spent his whole life in Słupca, although he did once make an appearance at our house in Pruszków. By then he was no longer young; I remember him as a tall, thin man, slightly yet unmistakably hunchbacked. I was three or at most four years old and decidedly ill disposed toward this old man who wanted me to sit on his lap. I don't know why he evoked fear in me. Only after some time did I grow accustomed to his presence, and even then only for a short time, for soon thereafter he elicited my terror when, unexpectedly, he donned a small, round cap, such as Orthodox Jews wear. He was not Orthodox, but he did live within the Jewish tradition, in accordance with its laws, and it may have been the Sabbath. In my parents' home we did not observe religious laws; even so, this was no reason why an older man, even one not particularly religious, would not remain faithful to them. I really don't know why it was that from the moment he put on a skullcap, he appeared threatening, bizarre, alien to me—and completely other than he had been a moment before.

The reactions of small children are strange and difficult to anticipate, so there's no reason for me to ponder my behavior at any length. I'll say only that this sudden terror must have been very intense, given that it has remained among the most vivid memories from my early childhood.

Sadly I don't remember my grandfather from our time in the ghetto, though I must have seen him at least every once in a while. I don't even know how it was that he found himself behind those walls in Warsaw, a city with which nothing had previously connected him. I don't know if all the Jews from Słupca were transferred there, or if he made an effort to join his family (he had been a widower for at least a quarter century). He lived with his oldest daughter, known in the family by her Polonized name Zosia, at the other end of the ghetto, and so—given the conditions of a sealed, maximally congested space—far away. I once paid a visit there with my father, which has stayed in my memory. I can still see Zosia's husband, by then very ill, lying in great pain, his legs swollen. (It seems he did not manage to die before being transported to Treblinka.) Yet my grandfather I don't remember, although he must have been there.

All I have written up to now has been merely foregrounding for reflecting upon his last act, an act to which I often return in my thoughts to reflect upon. To reflect upon, not recount, as I know too little of the related circumstances to be able to tell his story. In late July or early August 1942—I don't know the precise date, but it was definitely after the Germans had commenced the transports to Treblinka—my grandfather committed suicide. He threw himself from the third or fourth floor, he threw himself effectively, as he died at once. I remember how the news reached that distant end of the ghetto where we were living, and how my father took care of the burial. I'm consciously not saying "funeral," because when transports were leaving Umschlagplatz for Treblinka, there were no longer funerals in the normal sense of the word. Corpses were tossed into a collective grave in the Jewish cemetery, this is where my grandfather's body lies as well. I don't know if anyone accompanied my father in carrying him to that large hole where they tossed the fortunate ones, the ones who managed to die here, where they were, the ones who spared themselves the gas chambers.

I would give a lot today to discover the intellectual and emotional process that brought my grandfather to this decision. At the moment he made it, he was already an old man. I'm unsure of the exact date of his birth; I do know, though, that he came into this world at the beginning of the eighth decade of the nineteenth century, and so at a time when not even the most pessimistic of visionaries could have imagined a world where people were murdered *en masse* in gas chambers. I once reflected on this: the Holocaust also touched those born in the nineteenth century, or rather, more succinctly, people of the nineteenth century, who drew from that era their attitudes and prejudices, their ways of being in and perceiving the world. Three decades of my grandfather's life fell within that century, although I don't know if he could be called a man of the nineteenth century, such a definition would perhaps be misleading. My grandfather had not engaged with the great ideas of this bygone century, nor was he versed in its wonderful literature. He was, rather, an unexceptional provincial merchant occupied with his own affairs, who raised children and worked so that his modest enterprise would secure his family's material existence. He must have seen very little of the world outside of Słupca and its immediate environs; an occasional trip to Poznań constituted the most significant departure from his daily routine. My grandfather was a simple man, a petty bourgeois Jew with only an elementary education, and it is just when I think of his unassuming disposition and lack of distinction that his last gesture acquires a special meaning.

Thus I would give a lot to know how he came to that final decision. Did he reach the conclusion that there was no longer any hope? My grandfather, Lajzer Głowiński, levelheaded, well-mannered, in some way religious, and already past seventy, was old and sickly and could not count on living to see the end of the war and returning to a normal life—either in Słupca or anywhere else. Perhaps his decision was exclusively a personal one, yet it seems to me that it disclosed as well a broader field of reference, even if only by the moment at which it was realized. During the Holocaust there were no private suicides. Every death, and especially such deaths, in some way rendered themselves part of a public realm. I cannot claim that my grandfather understood precisely what the transports to Treblinka meant, or realized this was not about labor camps or resettlement in the East. Yet neither can I exclude the possibility that he harbored no illusions and saw before him only a disdainful, exhausting death. He wanted to spare himself this, and so chose that which, even in extreme conditions, he still could: he brought death to himself. He recognized that in the era of the Final Solution, the best solution for him was suicide. He was right, for he had no chance of survival; all possibilities of rescue were foreclosed to him. He might only have managed to gain a few days' delay, and so, with great effort, put off the final road to Umschlagplatz from, say, a Monday to a Friday. Such a delay was not worth the exertion, all the more so as it would have come without any hope in an even slightly extended future. It was difficult to harbor doubts that the end really meant the end. Expediting one's own end was an act of freedom, at that time more or less the only possible one. And inside the vanishing ghetto my grandfather carried out such a decision.

I think of this with the highest admiration, all the more so as I realize that a suicide carried out in such circumstances acquires a particularly symbolic meaning. I am persuaded that there is something impressive in attempting, as this elderly man did, to take one's own life. It belongs to those acts that, by the very fact of arising from free will, question what could be called the logic of the Holocaust. By the very act of suicide, the one condemned to death negates his sentence and asserts his moral independence, and this holds true even if that act results from desperation. I don't know whether suicides occurred frequently in the Warsaw Ghetto; I suspect no statistics were gathered. Moreover, suicides might have had one meaning in an earlier period and another during the final stage, when trains from Umschlagplatz were heading for Treblinka.

In short, I think of my grandfather's suicide, carried out at a time marked by extermination, as a heroic act, an act of the highest moral, existential, and human expression. This man understood that in the situation in which he found himself, together with millions of others similarly condemned, the only available means of deciding one's own fate, and so the only available means of freedom, was self-inflicted death—death by choice. If I were to write my family history, or attempt to weave a family legend, I would devote much space to my grandfather, who could not be murdered as he preferred to take his own life. I would devote much space to him, even though I knew him only vaguely and remember him only faintly. Admittedly my memories of him from before the war, from my earliest, idyllic childhood, bear no relationship to that final act, nor in any way foreshadow it. Yet memories neither subordinate themselves to strict logic nor conform to a hierarchy of importance. Then, in the late 1930s, neither I, not more than four years old, nor anyone could have suspected this modest provincial merchant of being capable of such an act. It is also true that in those years, even as danger rapped at the door, no one could have suspected that someone would set in motion gas chambers so as to murder by industrial methods.

In the context of the Holocaust one often hears of "death with dignity"—and sometimes one hears of foolish, thoughtless judgments. Everyone who died as a result of those criminal decrees died with dignity—and that must be said even when acknowledging the justness of Shakespeare's Brutus, who comments in *Julius Caesar,* just before making an attempt on his own life, "Our enemies have beat us to the pit: / It is more worthy to leap in ourselves, / Than tarry till they push us." There were only different styles of dying: the styles of the victims who could be delivered to the gas chambers without protest, and the styles of those who preferred to die actively. Some of those, like the ghetto fighters, put up resistance, others committed suicide. A person as old as my grandfather could choose only suicide.

❈

Beans and a Violin

It was when my parents first began working at Toebbens's shop. By this time I had become a sufficiently aware observer and participant to understand the associations carried by this word, which was part of the special vocabulary of the ghetto and most likely failed to bear such meaning either before or afterward; neither was the name Toebbens unfamiliar to me, if only because I heard it so often. Finding work there, where the only kind of work was slave labor, brought the hope of eluding the transports, and so the possibility of—even if only the possibility of thinking about—survival. Every day my parents set out for there, at times they spoke of it, yet for me Toebbens's shop remained a place distant and obscure. I was never there, I knew neither where it was nor what it looked like, I wouldn't know where to place it on a map of the shriveling ghetto. My sole enclave remained the apartment, the one room where we had now lived for a longer time. Although the apartment stood just by the walls, even after the *Aktion,* which had among its results the reduction of the ghetto's area, it remained within the ghetto's borders. It was in the nooks and crannies of that apartment that I was to hide as danger drew nearer. Often I was there alone, even though my parents did what they could to work different shifts at the shop.

The apartment had once been full of people; many had found shelter there. This was changing at the time I am now describ-

ing, around the end of the first phase of transports. I could tell
of the considerable movements among residents in that apartment, various people did not return, having set off from Umschlagplatz on a final path, one leading directly to the gas chambers. Several succeeded in getting through to the Aryan Side. I
remember but a few of them. Pani Franka has remained in my
mind. Not long before she had lost her only child, a boy my age
or younger, my family had known her before the war. She survived, and continued to use her occupation-era name after the
war, until the end of her long life she went by Pani Natalia. An
unnamed woman who lived in this apartment for a short time
lingers in the far reaches of my memory. This is so as the result of
a single story, and perhaps even a single sentence. She was telling
of a selection; a certain Jew, her acquaintance from before the
war, was assisting the Germans in conducting it. She sighed with
deep conviction—"What a decent man"—for when the German
pointed to her, her Jewish acquaintance suggested that another
woman be chosen instead, and so that time she was spared.

The mechanisms of memory intrigue me, those mechanisms
that caused just such words to be inscribed and in some sense
preserved forever, while so many other things that happened and
were said have vanished, impossible to re-create. I'm unable to
explain this phenomenon, for I didn't realize at the time just
how terrible was the remark that woman had just uttered. The
moral reflections of a child not yet eight years old cannot em-
brace the implications of such a statement. A child is not able to
consider, in evaluating the attitudes and behavior of those around
him, how the surrounding reality influences the shaping of criteria, and how that reality forces people to think in categories that
would never have come into being during more propitious times.
It nonetheless remains true that this comment in particular I did
remember, even though it need not have interested me at the
time. This was true all the more so as I never saw that Jewish collaborator and knew neither his name nor the identity of "this
other woman."

I will tell here not the story of that woman, of whose fate I know nothing. I don't know if she succeeded in saving herself from Treblinka. Rather, I want to tell of three sisters who, for a very short time, occupied one of the rooms in the apartment where we were living. I remember their name: it was Urstein. Their brother, who died at the very beginning of the occupation, was a well-known musician. There is an entry devoted to him in *The Small Encyclopedia of Music:* "Urstein, Ludwik, born 1874 in Warsaw, died 5 October 1939, also in Warsaw. Polish pianist and pedagogue. Studied at the conservatory in Warsaw. Distinguished accompanist and chamber musician."

That musician, appreciated among other things for his numerous appearances on Polish radio, had the good fortune to die at the right moment and so elude the ghetto and its torments. But this fate befell his sisters. I remember what they looked like: they wore black and very much resembled one another, to me they appeared old, although they were probably not past middle age. I never exchanged even a word with them; they kept to themselves and didn't initiate contact with their housemates. I associate them with stillness and silence. They spoke only among themselves, and in a whisper, perhaps to preserve their privacy, or perhaps, having been so crushed by misfortune, they preferred to bear their suffering within the confines of the family and were not capable of maintaining other relationships—even with those who, like they themselves, had been condemned to torment and humiliation, to the loss of those closest to them, and to relentless anticipation of death.

About these women I'm unable to say anything concrete. I don't know if they had ever married or if they were widows, I don't know if they once had families of their own and lost them with the ghetto's liquidation, I don't know if they had always been so close, or if only their time behind the walls had created this intimacy. In any case they have remained in my memory as always together, as three black figures who together left the apartment for Toebbens's shop and together returned. And one day, again together, they did not return. It was difficult not to surmise what had happened. They had been selected for the transport, there being no "decent man" to save them. Of course I don't know how it happened. Perhaps those carrying out the selection chose all three that day and condemned them to death in the gas chambers. Perhaps they called for only one, and the remaining two volunteered on their own, having decided not only to live, but also to die, in the company of family. In such situations people generally speak of a secret's being taken to the grave, yet in this case such a phrase would be an empty one—the murdered Jews took their secrets to the gas chambers.

And thus the Urstein sisters, whom today very few people— and perhaps no one apart from myself—remember, took their secrets to the gas chambers. And even I conjure them up in a particular way, as one evokes figures from childhood, even the most macabre one. It's an impoverished remembrance from which can be drawn only very little: they lived, and they died. . . .

They left behind a locked room, and what I will relate now is connected to this room. They no longer had any family to look through and take possession of what they had left behind. In this way the room into which they had moved not long before became an ownerless space; anyone who so wished could take for himself what had still been theirs the day before. In the ghetto during the liquidation most rights ceased to obtain; so too the right to property, held sacred by many not long before, lost its meaning. Both the valuable and the worthless could become no one's, as could personal keepsakes so dear to someone just the day before.

A certain young man, unknown to anyone in the apartment, was clearly aware of this. Several days after the Urstein sisters had disappeared, he materialized, claiming they had left behind a valuable violin, which he now wished to take. Initially he was questioned: what right did he have to it? This must not have been a very in-depth investigation, given that the unfamiliar man presented no evidence to support his claim. People did talk with him, though; the instrument might now just as well belong to him as to anyone else. The Urstein sisters' room was locked, and they had taken the keys with them on their final journey, it was necessary to open the door by some other means. The door was not forced from its frame, it gave way easily, almost without effort. And the violin was actually sitting there on display. The person who had come for it claimed it was old and valuable; he called it Ludwik Urstein's Violin. But had Ludwik Urstein actually played it? He was, after all, a pianist who accompanied violins, not a virtuoso of that instrument. Perhaps the violin had belonged to one of the sisters and she had played it? I don't know, of course, what the situation was, I don't know who the man was who took the violin, I don't know what happened to it. Perhaps it succeeded in escaping from the ghetto, for at that time it was needed there by no one. During the season of transports, when the central point behind the walls was Umschlagplatz, no longer did anyone play anything. Perhaps it succeeded in getting out just like those fleeing from extermination to the Aryan Side. Perhaps it survived and—if it really was such a good violin—is today serving some musician who plays Bach and Beethoven on it, unaware of its dramatic history. Yet perhaps it was destroyed, perished in that terrible meaning of the word "perish," which had become axiomatic at that time, perished together with the young man who considered that after the disappearance of its owners it should belong to him. Possibly he was a violinist himself who, during the last days of his life, wanted to play on a decent instrument.

I could continue to imagine scenarios for a long time, but I would prefer to relate what I do remember. In these stories about the ghetto, I am unconcerned with possible worlds; what interests me is what might have seemed impossible only a short while before, yet which had nonetheless become reality, the most horrifying reality among possibilities unthinkable just two or three years earlier. The room left behind by the Urstein sisters was undoubtedly real; now it belonged to no one and was available to anyone who wished to enter it. My father entered, and I with him. I'm uncertain when this took place, if it was just after the man departed with the violin, or somewhat later. For me, kept in the apartment and not having seen the outside world or done anything entertaining for a long time, it was definitely an attractive diversion to see something new, or at least something I had not seen in its present form, since I had been in that room before the three sisters moved there.

They had lived there barely a few days and had not yet managed to set up their home, everything was left out in disarray. Perhaps they chose not to organize things, conscious as they were that it would be a provisional deathbed arrangement, that any efforts at organizing things and putting down roots—if such was possible—would amount to self-deception on their deathbeds. That the room was virtually bare of furniture also contributed to the disarray. The room conspicuously lacked a cupboard, and so lying out on surfaces were various objects necessary for even the most basic existence: some plates, maybe also some kitchenware, some articles of clothing. This was all the sisters had left behind. The disarray became a trace of life suddenly and violently interrupted, a life before which there was no longer any chance.

Perhaps some remnants of food were left behind as well, and something that definitely amounted to a treasure: a bag with several kilograms of beans. This must have been a reserve the sisters had been saving for a black hour, a moment of greater hunger. I remember that in the ghetto, beans were an especially valued food. Now this treasure, like the violin, was without an owner; it belonged to no one. My father took it, and we ate the beans for some time, separating them sparingly into portions so that they would last.

Not long afterward, our belongings as well became no one's. We abandoned the room, leaving everything behind. I don't know if someone managed to make use of those things, among them was nothing to eat. We abandoned the room, and it was our good fortune not to be driven to Umschlagplatz and the ovens of the crematoria—we made our way to the Aryan Side.

※

Getting Out

I draw on this expression because there is no other within
my reach that would seem more appropriate. "Escape" feels still
less adequate, although of course it possesses that wonderful quality of evoking the biblical world. I would avoid using the word
"exodus," since in relation to events of this kind it would sound
lofty and pretentious. And when speaking of a terrifying world,
one of the most terrifying ever created, all sublime and ceremonial words are superfluous. Falsity creeps into them. Even the
cruelest episodes of the Bible bear no comparison to the stories
comprising the Holocaust. Even where it does not shy from relating chilling, harrowing events, the Bible always sets down
certain values, it accepts the premise that there exists in the
world a certain order containing its own meaning. There was
nothing of this kind in the Holocaust, where an insidious order
obtained, and with respect to what bore on the rescue of human
life, contingencies—dark and impossible to grasp, to capture, to
systematize, to comprehend—played an enormous role.

That I've digressed into these general reflections here was
prompted by the phrase "getting out"; they might otherwise
just as well have appeared elsewhere among these stories. I don't
know why there came into being the linguistic convention of
"getting out of the ghetto," while no one spoke of "getting out
of a concentration camp"—and this held in reference to a dra-

matic escape involving the highest of risks, as well as in reference to a person's release (which of course in the case of the Jews
was unimaginable). It came to pass that we—my parents and
I—got out of the ghetto at the very beginning of January 1943,
perhaps the very day after New Year's. We got out as the last of
those family members who had lived together and formed a
unified whole behind the ghetto walls. I'm speaking not of my
grandparents who, even before the transports, found themselves
on the Aryan Side due to a pure coincidence, a coincidence that
revealed itself to be unexpectedly generous toward them. I'm
thinking of my two aunts, each of whom left with her children,
and of their husbands—both of whom extricated themselves
from the space behind the walls somewhat later, and were killed
shortly thereafter.

Those in our family, from both my mother's and my father's
side, who lived in other parts of the ghetto did not get out—and
did not escape with their lives. They got out of the ghetto on
a final journey, directly to Treblinka. On which days and under
precisely what circumstances is unknown. When what must have
been complicated attempts were made to contact them, we were
told they were no longer there. They were, they existed, they
lived—and they were gone. No one could indulge in illusions,
it was clear what had happened. I cannot say whether news of
this sort engendered the kind of reaction normally elicited by
funeral announcements. After all, in a society being deliberately
and systematically murdered, was mourning possible in the
form it takes during (even only slightly) more normal times?
When one death follows another, and death threatens everyone,
and each person individually, it becomes difficult to contemplate
it. If reflections are possible at all, they are so only in the space
of a moment, not in larger spaces of time.

And so, of those in our family who succeeded in evading annihilation, it was we who remained in the ghetto the longest. I
don't know what played a role in this. Perhaps circumstances
were not propitious, or perhaps it was difficult to reach a decision—and the decision was a nontrivial one: one had to consider

the risk incurred in crossing the heavily guarded border that ran through the center of the city. Nor was it a secret that, once on the other side, one could quickly and easily fall into the hands of the *szmalcownicy,* which meant subjection to blackmail and perhaps death.

My father organized our departure, and he did it well, the process moved swiftly and efficiently. Unlike my aunt, we did not cross to the other side through the sewer canals. (Had it fallen to me to escape via an underground route, I would undoubtedly ascribe to that the fear of enclosed spaces I've suffered from in varying degrees of intensity since my adolescence.) I don't know how my father arranged it, and I'm never to learn. I did not ask him about the details, nor can I be certain that he had preserved them in his memory. Like many among the fortunate who survived the war, he avoided recollections, most likely suppressing them. Perhaps this was one of the conditions of returning to an ordinary, banal daily life, in which even serious problems were of a human dimension. It was not a simple task to realize this objective—to get from one part of the city to the other—which, to those locked behind the walls, appeared the domain of freedom and normality despite the fact that it, too, was under occupation and terrible things happened there. Getting out involved crossing the border marked by the wall, but it further required making arrangements on the Aryan Side so as not to land in a void, so as not to fall at once into undesirable hands and thus into a situation from which there was no getting out, even though it was precisely the result of getting out.

We got out together, all three of us, in a precarious way—but at that time everything was precarious, the risk in saving a life was life itself. We got out in a precarious, yet also—and here I must use this very inappropriate word—"luxurious" way. We passed through the gate separating the ghetto from the Aryan Side in a car driven by a German soldier. It was still dark when we left, things happened quickly, I probably never saw either the soldier or the car, which I don't remember, I only know it was not a truck, yet neither was it a passenger car in the strict sense of the word; it was covered with a tarpaulin and could have been some kind of military vehicle the Germans had at the time. We were to sit crouched in the back, dressed so as to be least conspicuous.

Our getting out was preceded by a certain event. I'm unaware of how my father brought about our departure; I do remember, though, that he arranged the matter with a man, no longer young, by the name of Kryształ. During this final phase in the ghetto, Kryształ performed some function, he must have been an official in contact with the Germans. I know nothing about him and cannot say whether he worked on behalf of the perishing society or was a collaborator, perhaps collaborating with the Germans in the hopes of saving his own life and the lives of those close to him. However the matter stood, it was he who mediated, he who arranged our departure. He knew a German soldier (there was one such soldier, and perhaps several) who was willing, under certain conditions and for a price, to transport Jews across the ghetto's border. He insisted they not have a Semitic appearance, and if I'm not mistaken, he charged Kryształ with making that judgment. Apparently he had confidence in Kryształ's discernment in this matter and trusted the criteria Kryształ applied; he must have judged that a Jewish eye would better be able to assess "bad looks" than his own German gaze. Moreover it's possible that, for reasons of safety, he preferred not to meet those to whom he was to render such an important service.

In connection with Kryształ's role as selector, something happened for the first time in several months: I left the apartment. He had already met my father and seen my mother at Toebbens's shop; it remained for him to see me to determine what I looked like, that is, whether there was anything of the stereotypical Jew in me. It was already dark when we met. I don't remember where it took place, yet Kryształ himself has stayed in my memory. He was not very tall, with hair entirely gray and a closely trimmed beard. For a long time my father discussed something with him, I listened to their conversation in a state of tension, as I came to understand what the important thing was over which they were bargaining. They must have agreed on some particulars—the day and place where we were to appear immediately after the curfew—and negotiated the size of the payment. They clearly reached some kind of compromise. Kryształ must have lowered the price somewhat, and perhaps as a reward for this my father paid him the compliment: "You are a true crystal." Possibly this came after Kryształ had concluded that my appearance was sufficiently un-Semitic so as to allow for a positive verdict, and so the mysterious and anonymous soldier would agree to transport us. If not, I think, for that play on words that imprinted itself on my memory, I would have forgotten his name. Even if he was a collaborator, he must not have played a very large role, since I haven't encountered his name in any of the histories of the Warsaw Ghetto I've since read.

In settling on a date, they also took into consideration precisely who would be standing watch at the ghetto's gates, the concern being that those on guard that day, even if not eager to allow anyone to get out, be sufficiently indifferent and uninquisitive so as to not take too much of an interest in who might be in the automobile. We sat in the backseat, crouched so as to be least visible; my mother wore a kerchief on her head, and I wore a thick woolen hat, called a pilot's cap, which covered much of my face. It had been bought for me before the war on Nalewki Street, at a children's clothing store called, if I'm not mistaken, U Franciszki. The pilot's cap grew, as if together with me, and served me well through several years of the war.

Most dramatic was passing through the gate. A soldier transporting such explosive cargo as a three-person family fleeing the ghetto naturally had to stop and present his documents to the guard. It didn't last long—the control check was of a routine nature—and we were quickly on our way. We got out at the agreed-upon place, somewhere downtown, most likely not far from the walls. It was still dark. How my father arranged this, how he managed to make contact with someone from the other side, I don't know, but there waiting for us was Długi, together with an unfamiliar man who, oddly enough, turned out to be a blue policeman. Thus we found ourselves on the Aryan Side. A new stage in my story began.

❖

Długi

I remember him from long ago, from that smallish fragment of my early childhood that was the mythical time "before the war." Every so often he would materialize at my parents' house, and his appearance was so distinctive that he immediately imprinted himself on my memory and awakened my imagination. He was very tall—he must have been well over six feet—and he spoke in an unusual, distinctive manner. Only later did I realize these things, for at the time such phenomena, for obvious reasons, didn't concern me. Yet it could not have escaped my attention that he walked with difficulty, shuffling his feet; that getting up from a chair was an obvious effort; that he didn't walk without a cane. It was said he was seriously ill. His difficulty in walking effected an astonishing contrast with his height, his great legs could not easily overcome even short distances and were of such little use. He belonged among those adults who did not ignore the presence of children. He paid obvious attention to me, and when he decided that I wasn't behaving as I should, he would speak to me in a didactic and seemingly threatening tone, though not in a way as to actually frighten me. It was the counsel of a person wise and experienced who warned me: "*Oy*, if you're naughty, Łojewski will come." Who this mysterious Łojewski was and what he would do to me I didn't know; the very prospect of his coming was supposed to call me to order. He was a mythical figure of my earliest childhood whom I remembered well and for a long time; when in writing for the underground press half a century later, I was faced with the necessity of choosing a pseudonym, I chose the name Łojewski. Of course my parents' guest could not have foreseen that in conjuring up a fictional character for my use, he created a myth I would turn to years later in circumstances entirely different and unfamiliar to him, as by then he had no longer been living for decades. He was called Długi, as if everyone had forgotten that his name was Józef. Thus he was always spoken of as well as addressed, and this must not only have been to distinguish him among the several Józefs in the family. He was my mother's cousin, older than she by more than a dozen years. The families of times past tended to be numerous—there were many cousins—yet I did not meet, or in any case do not remember, any apart from this one. Długi was a colorful, unique character with an uncommon biography. The oldest son of my grandfather's oldest sister Mechła, Długi was most likely born around the year 1890, and at a certain moment became an American citizen. The whole strange and unusual story is connected to this.

My grandfather's family descended from northern Mazowsze, in the vicinity of Płock, from a place named Bielsk, an unimaginably godforsaken hole. At the turn of the century the youngest generation left there to settle in the vicinity of Warsaw or Łódź or elsewhere still, I'm unfamiliar with the particulars, events from a century ago are now buried in oblivion and no longer is there anyone among the living who could provide reliable information. In any case, some time after her marriage and the birth of her son, Mechła settled in Pruszków; shortly thereafter two of her brothers moved there, one of whom was my grandfather. I know little about her married life. Family legend relates that her husband, like many young Jews in those times, wished to immigrate to America. Mechła, however, resolutely opposed this plan, perhaps because she feared she would be unable to manage in a new, strange world, or perhaps because she was unable to imagine life outside of a small Polish town (even one such as Pruszków, where there were not many Jews). This space was her own; it was domesticated and familiar. Her husband had his way, though, and in a rather original manner: one day he went to Warsaw—and never returned. Days passed, weeks, months, and he gave no sign of life. Poor Mechła didn't know whether to consider herself a widow, or rather—equally unfortunate—the abandoned mother of three children, left to her own fate. Either way, it was a scandal in a model petit bourgeois family. Only after several months did it come to light that she was neither widowed nor abandoned, but rather the wife of a man with dreams and ideas who aspired to realize them by any means—and who was irresponsible. A letter from New York told her that he had indeed immigrated to America and begun working, and that as soon as he had earned some money, he would send tickets for her and the children. He kept his word, and after some time Mechła, together with her daughter and two sons, set out across the ocean. They settled in Brooklyn, and Mechła lived to a venerable old age, dying a few years after the Second World War— and so did this mad, secret act of her husband save her from extermination. And Długi, like his parents and siblings, became an American citizen, the importance of which was revealed several decades later when he was living in a land where a savage history was playing itself out.

About his stay in America I know little. Once he reached adulthood, he worked as a canvasser for the famous Singer sewing machine company, known in Poland, too, at the time. I would guess he promoted the company in either Yiddish or Polish, as it's difficult for me to imagine his doing so in English. His Polish was odd—he spoke the bad Polish typical of Jews—and in it one could hear words borrowed from English as well. Yet Polish, like Yiddish, he had known since childhood, whereas he was immersed in English only as an adolescent. I'm willing to guess that his mastery of English was limited, and that he would not have had at his disposal the kind of knowledge that would have allowed him to promote Singer's products efficaciously to white Anglo-Saxon Protestants. He must have worked in Brooklyn.

He married early, it seems, and had a son. The marriage did

not last long. From the beginning it was disastrous because, he consistently maintained, he had happened upon a frightful woman. He called her "heksa," "the witch." And certainly it would not have lasted very long, if only because Długi treated every woman—provided she was not overly aged and looked tolerably well—as a challenge. In this realm he had tremendous needs and ambitions. All hell broke loose. There was a trial. The court granted a divorce and, holding Długi responsible for the disintegration of the marriage, sentenced him to pay a huge sum in alimony, disproportionately high—in his opinion—in relation to his earnings. He was forced to work exclusively so as to make the alimony payments, and this he had no desire to do. To liberate himself he did what his father had done years earlier: without telling his former wife and without saying goodbye to his son, he set off on a trip—only in the opposite direction, to Poland. He kept in touch with neither the witch nor their son. It might have seemed that he cared about nothing, perhaps his hatred for his former wife had passed onto his son. Lacking in paternal instinct, Długi took no interest in him for many years and was unaware of his fate. He corresponded only with his parents and siblings, who were by then doing quite well in America; rather quickly his younger brother Tobiasz began to grow prosperous.

I'm unable to situate these events precisely in time, I'm certain of only one thing: when Długi returned to Poland, it was still the 1920s. When he left Poland after the war, he left my parents a photo album, which is now with me. In it there's a photograph of my mother with her sister Maria, three years younger, in Długi's company in Zakopane. This photograph is of special value to me, as it's one of the few that has survived from my mother's maidenhood, it must have been taken around 1930.

After his return, Długi grew close to my grandparents and regarded their house in Pruszków as his family home; he was there often, and I suppose lived there for some time. He was one of those people whose presence is always welcome, he was well liked for his directness, his imagination, and his sense of humor, even though his way of being posed a distinct contrast to the strict atmosphere and highly rigid principles obtaining in that house. Długi, a divorced man with an unsettled personal life who was perpetually engaging in new romances—rumors of which supplemented his own accounts—and who was in an unstable position in every respect, was a strange creature set against the backdrop of my grandparents' uncommonly solid and orderly world. I believe it speaks well of my grandparents that they not only tolerated him, but further, beginning at a certain moment, began to treat him as the closest of kin. And this tie grew stronger still when it became known that Długi was seriously ill, that he was afflicted with a terrible, debilitating disease, which rendered him vulnerable to long-lasting suffering and the progressive loss of various abilities. That, however, is another story.

After his return to Poland, Długi had to begin everything anew. He faced some fundamental decisions: what to do, where to live, how to find a place for himself in life. For a time he found a haven in Pruszków, although I don't know what kind of work he did there. At a certain moment he made a decision that might have seemed whimsical and reckless: he would settle down in the country and buy a bit of land with the money he had brought from America. No one had anticipated this course of events, there were no agricultural traditions in our family, and until then Długi himself had no experience in growing crops or raising livestock. Like everything in his life, this decision seemed irresponsible, indeed mad. Yet Długi did effect its realization, purchasing almost fifty hectares from Earl Sobański. I don't know who this Earl Sobański was, though he recurred frequently in Długi's reminiscences and, like most people appearing in the stories Długi enjoyed conjuring up on various occasions, Earl Sobański took on a mythical persona. Moreover, that the property was just short of fifty hectares later revealed itself to be of much significance: it was not subject to the 1945 law on agricultural reform.

The estate was located in R., a large village on the railway line between Żyrardów and Skierniewice. Długi settled there and set to work; he employed a few people, yet decided that the estate as a whole he would manage himself. I would suppose, in the beginning, he made one mistake after another; somehow he did accustom himself to the work, although, as I've heard, he never did achieve significant results. Moreover, his employees and neighbors quickly figured out that he was unversed in matters agricultural and accordingly did as they pleased, persuading him of various fantastical stories and exposing him to losses. I'm unable to say very much about that estate, as I saw it when it was already verging toward decline, and when Długi, after the war, was preparing for a return journey to the United States.

His terrible disease manifested itself during the interwar years. The first sign was difficulty in walking, shortly thereafter the doctors pronounced a diagnosis: *sclerosis multiplex*. He described it this way, and it was thus spoken of, as at that time the Polish version of the term "multiple sclerosis," while perhaps used among specialists, had not yet entered the colloquial language. He suffered very much and moved only with difficulty, yet even so the disease took a relatively mild course, and he survived with it and led an active life for over thirty years. It seems that only in its final stage did the disease reveal itself in its full awfulness, but this came after he had returned to America, and so at a time when those of us here knew little about him.

He underwent treatment here, but every year went to Austria to take a cure. In the album I've mentioned are his photographs from Baden, where he went to the spa. Most often he was photographed amid a chaplet of women. One—young, attractive, dressed according to the mandates of interwar fashion—reappears in several photographs. This must have been Herta, his longtime Austrian lover, about whom he often reminisced. Of these erotic conquests there were many; notwithstanding his serious illness, he was constantly augmenting their number— and not only at the spa outside of Vienna. He would also travel to Łódź, where, as I understand, he was involved with a lady of allegedly less than noble virtues. Nor was he idle in this realm in his own village—a serious matter, during his last years in Poland he was involved with a girl he employed to keep house.

He spent his time in Baden not only courting the pretty Herta, but also taking advantage of the attractions of cultural life. My mother mentioned that he once told her (it must have been in the mid-1930s) of going with Herta to concerts in Baden where they played grandiose symphonies by a composer still unknown in Poland, by the name of Mahler. Thus my mother heard that name for the first time, and when shortly thereafter she came upon his Fourth Symphony on Polish radio, she already knew who this man was. It's difficult for me to say whether Długi was deeply interested in music or other spheres of art, or whether his encounter with Mahler was the result of chance, or of the influence of his Austrian lover who enjoyed monumental symphonies. Whatever the case, the anecdote has been preserved of his having gone, as a teenage boy, with a friend to see the opera *Halka* at Teatr Wielki. He was sold tickets, yet when he appeared in a sheepskin coat and not especially clean riding boots, the ushers didn't want to admit him to the performance. Poor Długi did not see Moniuszko's opera that time. He was very young, and didn't know that going to the theater involved wearing something a bit more formal and conventional.

At a certain point, quite easily calculated historically, his yearly trips to Austria came to an end. First came the *Anschluss,* and what happened afterward is well known. When the war broke out, it seems that Długi did not even try to return to America; he decided to stay on his estate in R. It was not his lot to remain there, and the Germans expelled him, allocating his property to a *Treuhänder,* a role filled by a *Volksdeutsche* from Poznań, one bearing a Polish surname I remember to this day: Pawlak. Yet Długi did not, at least not for some time, abandon the village, he did not leave R. For it was just then, at the very beginning of the war or perhaps just slightly before, that he became involved with Natka (this odd name must have been a diminutive from Natalia). I'm unable to reconstruct the precise chronology, and there is no longer anyone who could assist me. Perhaps Natka is still living—she would be an elderly woman of more than eighty—yet I would not be able to find her, even if I were to try. I know neither her maiden nor her married name (for in the end, as we shall see, she did marry). It would be searching for a breeze in a field, a breeze from many decades ago. Długi took her on when it was still peacetime. She must have kept house later as well, but soon her role was to change radically, to become incomparably more significant. Until the end of Długi's stay in Poland, she was his lover, something she did not keep a secret, which in the provincial society she had come from must have been the occasion for much talk and gossip—and when in his old age he became increasingly decrepit, it was she who cared for him. She played an active role, too, when Długi was helping to rescue his family, extricating them from behind the ghetto walls. Natka's record during the occupation years is a noble one. When in late November or early December 1943 the area grew dangerous—the Germans had caught and shot several Jewish families hiding there—my mother and I found a week's shelter in a potato heap, part of a tiny property belonging to Natka's family. And it was she who, each morning and evening, let us out for a short while so as to allow us to take care of bodily functions and who brought us food. Długi had complete confidence in her, he confided all of his secrets to her, and as is apparent drew upon her help in hiding those who had managed to get out of the ghetto.

In fact people were astonished that he had gotten involved with her in particular. She was far from being a buxom village beauty, it was difficult to hide that she was ugly and at once unpleasant, sharp, and domineering. It was said—and it seems, not unjustly—that she took him by the pants and at least from a certain moment did just as she pleased. In any case she must have distinguished herself by some qualities difficult to perceive from afar, given that he did choose her in particular and spent a large part of his life with her. Długi did not go to the ghetto and did not wear the armband with the Star of David, and it was she who was with him during the years of the occupation.

Długi fit perfectly the Nazi criteria for being a Jew, yet until a certain time he was not in hiding: he lived on the Aryan Side, although it would certainly be difficult to say he lived normally.

This was undoubtedly decided by the American passport, of which he was the fortunate owner. Jews possessing American citizenship were also, after all, imprisoned in the ghetto, though their chances of survival were relatively greater, as Mary Berg relates in her moving diary. If I'm not mistaken, he somehow made several appearances in the Warsaw Ghetto to visit family, yet he was a guest from another world, and his relationship with the ghetto lay in his helping to extricate family members from behind the walls when the *Aktion* commenced—after the terrible day of 22 July 1942—and on one occasion even before that.

This occasion concerned my grandparents. That they survived the war they owe to a bit of good fortune and above all to Długi. I confess that I consider their survival, against all probability, to be one of the miracles of the occupation years; if I were a believer, I would write that God had taken them under his special protection, a protection he begrudged millions of others. They were elderly (having been born in the mid- or late-1870s), already very sickly, yet still functioning tolerably well. Moreover, the issue here is not only one of mathematical age—during ghastly times, people age more quickly, with the years accruing at double or triple the usual speed. And here I'm unable to refrain from a digression about the fate of the elderly, who had no chance of survival during the Holocaust. For years I've thought of the Holocaust as a slaughter carried out against those born in the nineteenth century, an enormous mass of people shaped in that century, living by the imaginations and ideas they absorbed in that era. A slaughter of those for whom the idea of murder by industrial methods was beyond comprehension for the simple reason that it transcended the boundaries of their technological imagination. Sometimes I ask myself when the nineteenth century ended for Jews, and I think it was not at the moment it did for others, when the First World War began, but rather at the moment when the crematoria in Treblinka, Auschwitz, and other such places designated for genocide were set in motion.

It was largely by chance that my maternal grandparents escaped the transports from Umschlagplatz and the ovens in Treblinka, thanks to something that appeared to be and really was ill fortune, but an ill fortune that spared them a greater, and final, one. My grandmother was rapidly losing her vision, and blindness drew nearer with each passing day. The ophthalmologist pronounced that the process could be halted only by an operation, an operation that could not be performed in the conditions of the ghetto; it could be done only on the Aryan Side. After much vacillation and deliberation, and meticulous consideration of finances, my grandparents decided that somehow they would leave the ghetto; they would spend about two weeks on the other side of the wall, as this was the time needed for everything connected with the operation, and then they would return. For various reasons, medical and otherwise, the operation failed, my grandmother was plunged into total darkness and never regained her sight. Yet my grandparents never did return to the ghetto. When the time approached for them to make their way back, it—that is, the *Aktion,* the liquidation, the transports—had begun.

That they got out was thanks to Długi. Not only was he waiting for them at the designated spot on the Aryan Side, but he also organized the entire difficult and dangerous undertaking. My grandparents spoke Polish well; they further distinguished themselves by their so-called "good looks," this was especially true of my grandfather who, with his moustache and crop of gray hair, resembled more a country squire than a Jew from a small town near Warsaw. Even so the risks were enormous. I'm not familiar with the details, I don't know what their lives were like during the first days of their stay *extra muros,* yet one thing is certain: it was Długi who took care of them. He found them a refuge when it became clear that it no longer made sense to return to the ghetto. It was he who procured fictitious documents for them and placed them with a peasant family he had befriended in one of the hamlets adjoining R., where he was then still living. It was he who, together with Natka, was in constant contact with them, appearing with assistance when necessary. It was he who, when that area became especially dangerous, organized their escape from R., and he who arranged their move to Milanówek, where a hiding place awaited them.

In the area where Długi lived, two more cousins were hiding, together with their families; they were the daughters of my grandfather's oldest brother. That they found themselves there was also undoubtedly thanks to Długi. They, however, did not succeed in surviving the war: both families, in two separate places, were discovered and shot. This was after my grandparents had fled those parts, and when my mother and I, after having hidden for a week in the potato heap, crept one day at dawn in complete darkness to the railway station in R. to take the first train to Warsaw. This was late autumn 1943, when someone had passed on the information that there were Jews hiding in several villages, and the Germans had set about combing through the territory. More than a dozen people were killed.

That my mother and I were hiding in the Wolskis' small house in R., and my father several kilometers away in the home of a peasant, naturally came about thanks to Długi. (Kazimierz Wolski was a retired stationmaster in R. Some time after we had left, he was shot and killed by the Gestapo, not, however, for hiding Jews in his home, but rather for working in the underground—he was active in the Home Army.) Above all, Długi helped us when we were escaping from the ghetto. Among his acquaintances was a blue policeman, and Długi induced him to come for us immediately after we had gotten out and to keep us in his apartment for a day or two—that this occurred illustrates as well that not all blue policemen were alike. In this way we avoided the danger of roaming the streets, and found ourselves in a world to some extent prepared for our arrival—at least for the immediate following days.

At this time Długi, as an American citizen, could still move about relatively freely, although this would soon end. It's difficult for me to determine during which phase of the occupation this occurred; in any case, he, too, now had to go into hiding. And it was then that Natka revealed herself to be not only devoted to him, but also responsible, energetic, and resourceful.

I can say very little about this period of his life, as I was then far
away from Warsaw and no family stories have stayed in my
memory, most likely I was never told anything. In any case,
something else interests me more than concrete biographical
facts: the change that came over Długi during the occupation.
He had the reputation of someone reckless and irresponsible,
prone to fantasies and momentary whims, whose life and person
were in disarray, someone incapable of acting with exactitude
and seeing undertakings through to the end, interested primarily in his own small affairs and unlikely to concern himself with
matters affecting others. And suddenly it came about that in conditions for which, after all, no one had been prepared, he was able
to function energetically, to anticipate what might occur; he was
prepared to put himself at risk, to stake everything on a single
card to best help his family. And he proved himself to be responsible and capable of exploiting his imagination and inventive-
ness in conspiratorial activity (which included not only things
military and political, but also assistance in saving the lives of
those who succeeded in getting out from behind the walls). That
he was efficacious was linked to his ability to connect with
people, to engage their imaginations and win them over. The
war made him a different person, releasing inside him something the existence of which he himself must not have suspected.

What he did should be emphasized all the more so given that
he was seriously ill; his multiple sclerosis did not remain at the
stage it had reached in the beautiful years before the war. He
walked with greater and greater difficulty, and the disease's successive symptoms became apparent. He was in this state when
the liberation came. He returned to R. and regained his property,
yet then had to consider where to go with his life and what to do
next. Doubtlessly he was aware that he was becoming increasingly decrepit and that working on his land—which, after all,
had never been in good form and during the war had deteriorated
even further—surpassed his capabilities. He thought more and
more seriously about returning to America, all the more so as the
communist order coming into being in Poland provoked ever

greater anxiety—although he could not have known then, in 1946, that if he stayed he would soon be classified as a *kulak,* a class enemy against whom it was necessary to fight. It was then that he set off on his first postwar journey. He wanted to find out whether returning to New York after a twenty-year absence made any sense, whether he would manage to make a life for himself there after such a long time, and also—and this was an important question—whether he could count on the assistance of his family, whose position had improved considerably during this period. He wanted to see them, and in particular his mother, who was by then extremely aged. As far as I'm aware, making contact with his son was of the least importance to him; he had not taken part in his upbringing and in essence treated him like a stranger. (They must have met, but little came of it.) He believed, too, that American doctors could help him more effectively than Polish doctors could. He decided he would stay in America, returning to Poland only in order to close his affairs.

And immediately upon his return, he began the process of closure. There were complicated properties issues I know little about; I know that part of the farm he sold, part he allocated for outstanding mortgage loans, and part, perhaps even the largest part, he signed over to Natka. He had lived with her for many years, and in departing from the country forever must have thought about not leaving her with nothing, about somehow providing for her. In this sense he found himself under great pressure. She demanded what was due to her, I would suppose in an extremely forceful way, and Długi decided that not only would he bestow upon her many hectares of land, but he would also marry her off. He so began an energetic search for a candidate, and found one in a nearby village. It's true that this peasant didn't know Natka, had never even seen her, but the possibility of acquiring the rich dowry of land borne by this now-single woman was sufficiently compelling, and he made the decision. He did set one condition: his fiancée could not be older than he was—which unfortunately she was, and considerably. By then she was over thirty, an old maid not only by village custom,

while the land-hungry youth was barely past twenty. Długi
wanted his unusual matchmaking endeavor to meet with suc-
cess, and so set to work with redoubled energy. He tried to persuade the potential bridegroom, found with such difficulty, that
Natka was a young woman. Persuasion was insufficient, however—some kind of documentary proof was needed—and it was
critical above all to ensure that the intrigue would not be unmasked. With this goal he went to the parish priest, with whom
he had decent—if not good—relations, to ask him not to reveal
Natka's birthdate in the course of arranging the formalities or
later during the wedding ceremony. Initially the priest was re-
luctant, but Długi persuaded him in the end, arguing that if the
priest were to reveal the bride's age, the whole affair would fall
apart, and this would be unfortunate for all of them.

Marrying off Natka was Długi's last act on Polish soil. He did
what was his to do and set off on a journey, this time a final one,
to the other side of the Atlantic. As best as I can recall, he boarded
the *Batory* in Gdynia; at this time people did not yet travel across
the ocean by plane. He had grown old and sickly, and must have
realized that he would never again see Poland, where he had
spent a large part of his life. I know little about his fate in America. His family must have secured some kind of minimal existence for him. Perhaps they treated his arrival after so many years
like the return of a prodigal son, already decrepit, advanced in
years, verging toward the grave.

He had never been one to write letters; he sent two or three
after his departure, and then was silent. Perhaps his worsening
illness had not only attacked his legs; perhaps its destructive effects had also seized his arms, rendering him physically unable
to reach for a pen. Other considerations may also have come into
play—Stalinist terror was intensifying, and Długi might have
been concerned that contact with relatives in America could expose his family to repression.

I don't know the date of his death. I think he departed from
our vale of tears no later than the mid-fifties. No one told his
Polish family, even though he had been so close to them.

The Black Hour

I've told this story to various people, and I've long wanted to commit it to paper as a testimony of those times. Yet something always restrained me. In essence I was protecting myself from it, as if the act of transcription would summon those events back to life in all their horror. I confess that even now I take up the task with difficulty, I struggle against my resistance, yet I don't want this story to remain forever in my memory alone. Literary considerations also bore on my years of inability to overcome this reluctance. I worried that, against my will, this authentic narrative would conform to a certain paradigm, as after all there does exist an age-old topos, embodied most pointedly in iconography, but also in numerous verbal incarnations, depicting a man's contest with Death—a contest played, as a rule, with cards or dice for the highest stakes. In fact I played chess, and not with Death himself, but with a young man who had come to the decision to condemn me to death. A game of chess between a child and a *szmalcownik* might seem a trite literary device, a peculiar resurrection of an archaic motif, yet my story contains no fiction, no invented scenes, and if "literature" does emerge, it is merely derivative, inadvertent, and unintentional. The event I'm speaking of took place at a time when the most extraordinarily diabolical things could occur. And so they did.

In early 1943, shortly after we had gotten out of the ghetto, we found shelter as a threesome—my mother, my aunt Teodora, and I—in an attic on Srebrna Street, in the center of Warsaw. The house was old and in disrepair, and the attic was in a lamentable state. I don't know who found it for us, it seemed relatively safe, we hoped to avoid attracting attention and with luck to hide there for at least a bit of time. The attic was empty. There was no furniture save two stools, and the walls were stained with mildew. The electricity must have been shut off, and there was no heat—winters during the occupation were distinctive in their harshness—but rather only a so-called "goat," a cast-iron stove with a long pipe, which served as an oven. We slept on straw-filled mattresses. These primitive conditions did not elicit complaints, the important thing was that we had a refuge. Those four shabby walls rescued us from homelessness—and thus from being sent to a quick and certain death.

I was already eight years old and aware of my situation. Fear is an excellent teacher. It rapidly engenders a consciousness of one's position and fate, cures a child of fantasies and delusions, and precludes the development of childhood interests. I had much time, and because I could not fill this time in ways appropriate for someone of that age, I sunk into inactivity. There had been a certain period in the ghetto, before the beginning of the *Aktion* when no one yet spoke of Umschlagplatz and Treblinka, when I had begun to devour books. Yet on Srebrna Street I did not have a single printed word, with the exception of a religious booklet someone had given me from which I was to learn some basic prayers, so that should it be necessary, I would be able to recite Our Father, Hail Mary, and the Apostle's Creed—and thus prove that I was not a Jew. Familiarity with the holy texts, a familiarity taken for granted for a Catholic, was treated as a test. This most likely was of no help to anyone, yet even so, on the Aryan Side these prayers were widely learned, as they were regarded as something in the way of a legitimation, or, at least in certain circumstances, as a last resort. I, too, learned them by heart. For me they carried no particular associations; they were rather nothing more than a sequence of sentences for obligatory memorization, and I absorbed them with indifference. I was intellectually stunted at the time, as if I had ceased to develop. In any case, at a certain dramatic moment the prayers I had crammed into my head without comprehension revealed themselves to be useless—our persecutor had no doubts as to who we were and no need to test anything. Even had I performed the most beautiful recitation of half the catechism, it would have mattered very little to him.

However I did have one thing to make a terrible time more bearable—a chess set. Earlier, when we were still in the ghetto, I had learned to play; just after the transports to Treblinka began, when I had begun to hide in various places, it became my main diversion. I mastered the fundamentals quickly, I don't remember who instructed me in them. Obviously, I had no partner. Someone had given me as a gift a thick book with descriptions of matches played by the great chess masters, and I replayed the famous matches on my own chessboard with enthusiasm, I was enthralled by their drama. I identified first with one player, then with the other. In the attic on Srebrna Street I no longer had that book, it had remained in the ghetto, there had been no way to take it when we slipped away from behind the walls. I did still have the small wooden chess pieces, which I kept in a tattered cardboard box (to this day I remember its faded blue color), together with the very bedraggled chessboard. And so I played chess against myself. I played for hours on end; it was my only pastime. Today I no longer understand how I managed to divide myself between two roles and sympathies, yet it remains true that this was my principal means of filling the infernal, empty hours. I couldn't venture out into the courtyard or play with other children, and I had no books—apart from that small religious booklet meant to teach me the most important prayers.

I was playing alone like this when someone knocked on the door. Unannounced and unexpected knocking portended nothing good, and what was now resounding was understood at once to be not friendly, but rather aggressive, loud, confident. Someone who knocks like this has come not to help, but to put you in your place. Fear paralyzed us, but in the end we opened the door, as otherwise it would have been broken down. In the best case it would be the building caretaker coming to evict us from the attic; after all, we were squatters with no registration, although we were paying to stay there. But it was not the caretaker. A stranger stood in the doorway, a young man dressed elegantly in accordance with occupation-era fashion. It was difficult to delude ourselves about his intentions. There was no doubt we were lost. We had to bid life farewell.

While still at the threshold, the fellow declared that he knew who we were and would hand us over to the Germans. Our efforts to convince him that he was mistaken—after all, our documents were all in order—were, like our entreaties, obviously of no use. The young man was unyielding, deaf to pleas and arguments. I don't know if I knew the word *"szmalcownik"* at the time; if not, it was precisely on that January day that I came to understand to what and whom it referred. It did not take long for the question of bribery to arise. We had neither money nor anything of value; the paltry few *groszy* each woman possessed at the moment of his intrusion would clearly not satisfy our uninvited guest, this money might have sufficed for two loaves of bread and a liter of milk. There was a dire need to find something immediately with which to ransom ourselves. My father, who was hiding at that time in another part of the city, still possessed a little money and the remaining jewelry, set aside for a black hour; these things comprised an essential reserve, and perhaps the price of our lives. It was difficult to imagine a blacker hour than this one; in the attic on Srebrna Street, the boundary between life and death had been nearly effaced, and the game was being played for the highest stakes. At the end of long negotiations, it was decided that Teodora would go into the city, contact someone, and return with the ransom, while my mother and I remained in the attic as hostages. The *szmalcownik* graciously expressed his consent.

We waited for a long time—I'm unable to say how many hours, but definitely a long time—and not only because time had expanded in our terror-laden waiting, for after all, we didn't know what would happen, whether Teodora would be successful in finding the ransom, and whether after procuring it the *szmal-cownik* wouldn't take us to the Gestapo all the same. We didn't know what kind of miscreant he was—whether he only cared about the money or whether he was also an anti-Semite by conviction, someone who saw the unmasking and persecution of Jews hiding on the Aryan Side as his mission. If we were dealing with an ideological *szmalcownik,* our chances of surviving his incursion would be nonexistent.

In the course of the prolonged waiting he sat down on one of the two stools. He did not take off his coat. It was cold in our attic; since his arrival, no one had tended to the cast-iron stove and the flame had gone out. To this day I still remember his overcoat, which was heavy and gray and made of material in a herringbone pattern. The workings of memory are curious: his winter attire has been preserved in my memory more deeply and lastingly than his face, which in all likelihood lacked distinctiveness, perhaps apart from a closely trimmed moustache, the kind popular physiognomy commonly ascribes to underworld characters. He sat calmly, not conversing with us, from time to time expressing his impatience at how the situation was dragging on and he was wasting his valuable time unnecessarily. He was clearly bored.

I was doing nothing. I sat vacantly on the mattress, yet it would be difficult to say I was bored—fear and terror don't engender boredom. I was a well-versed and seasoned Jewish child, I grasped our situation perfectly and knew what "we'll go to the Gestapo" meant. I harbored no illusions and was aware that this awful day could end in death. One could say literally that the quiet in the attic was grave. At a certain moment I saw the box of chess pieces sitting on the windowsill, and I laid out the chessboard on the mattress, but obviously was not in a state to play in any sensible manner. I moved the pieces around without rhyme or reason, just to wile away the dreadful waiting and to extricate myself, if only for a moment, from the oppression of the deathly quiet.

At a certain moment something unforeseen happened: the

bored *szmalcownik* proposed that we play a game of chess. I don't
remember how the match progressed or whose side might have
won, yet I do know that we didn't finish—as the match approached its conclusion, Teodora returned. From this moment
the *szmalcownik* was interested only in the prize for which he'd
been made to wait several hours. Initially he grew angry—there
was too little—but in the end, he took it and left us. I wanted
to write "he left us in peace," but I realized immediately that the
phrase would be unbefitting and would sound false—and not
only for the more general reason that we, the condemned, could
not experience peace for even a moment. It would sound deceptive as well in reference to this concrete situation, for we were
left to answer the dramatic question: what next?

Following the *szmalcownik*'s departure, it was obvious that we
should not remain in the attic even for a short time—the location was now exposed, or as people said then, "burnt." We could
not naively presume that the *szmalcownik* would not return a moment later or the next morning, nor could we dismiss the possibility that he would send along a friend and the whole scene
would begin anew. Only this time, there was no doubt that it
would end differently, for a subsequent black hour would be in-
disputably the final one. This was no longer a chess match, and
while the ending was easy to predict, it was harder to predict
what rules the *szmalcownik* would honor. Did he consider everything in his profession permissible, or was he an "honest" extor-
tionist, not thrusting himself a second time upon those from
whom he'd already extracted ransom?

We could not leave the attic on Srebrna Street that day. The
curfew was drawing near and to be found on the street would be
still more dangerous—it would mean immediate death. We had
nowhere to go, and so we persevered in our "burnt" residence
until dawn. As soon as the curfew ended, we set out. We had almost nothing. My mother and my aunt Teodora took some small
bundles, and I held the box with the chess set, with which I'd
played with someone who had no scruples about bringing a sentence down upon me though, to be sure, he himself would not

have been its executor. A new stage of flight from death began, most likely resulting more from an instinctual attachment to life than from a conscious faith in survival. That whole time, regardless of which side of the wall we found ourselves on, became one vast black hour, and if differentiations did reveal themselves, it was only in hues.

And with this thought I might close my story about what took place on a certain day in January 1943 *Anno Domini,* in the attic on Srebrna Street, yet I feel a need to say something more. I want to add that I still have the image of that *szmalcownik* before my eyes; I can still see that well-built young man, who had chosen the most abhorrent livelihood, for certainly it's possible to thus describe the blackmailing of those condemned to extermination. At times I treat him not only as a concrete person, but also—and perhaps above all—as a kind of empirical archetype of an occupation-era hyena. Every mention of *szmalcownictwo* draws from the depths of my memory precisely this fellow.

And a word more about chess. I took the chess set from Srebrna Street in its tattered cardboard box. I don't remember what happened to it or how I lost it; I think, though, that it disappeared shortly after we abandoned that attic of ill omen, during one of the next stages of my wanderings. And that I've forgotten is both significant and characteristic. Such a short while before the chess set had been an object of tremendous value, thanks to it, I was able to fill my time in hiding. Yet suddenly it ceased to interest me, I no longer needed it. My passion had abated, perhaps because I descended into a state of apathy. I was no longer drawn to anything, I no longer cared about anything, I entered a state of vegetation, of stupor, as if all intelligence and capacity for thought had dissolved within me. Yet I believe that what most influenced this sudden change was the chess match played against the *szmalcownik*—or rather, against Death, who on this occasion had assumed the form not of a skeleton with a scythe, but rather of a well-built young man with a roguishly trimmed moustache.

Candid Evening Talks

Any instance of unforeseen knocking—even the quietest, gentlest, most delicate knocking—elicited anxiety. It meant that something unexpected had taken place, unexpected and therefore not good, as in those times it was difficult to imagine that anything auspicious or fortunate could occur. It might be possible to generate a phenomenology of knocking; everything in it bore significance. Someone who came without harmful intentions, most often with a critical, urgent matter, one resulting from a sudden coincidence or requiring an immediate resolution, tended to knock in such a way so as not to frighten anyone. While needing to transmit a signal and elicit a response, he at once made it understood that he was not a German, a policeman, or a *szmalcownik*—they knocked in a different way, loudly and energetically, with no hesitation, and in this way revealed their intent. Knocking evolved into a kind of *carte de visite:* it was marked, it became a form of introduction. It was intended not only to compel an immediate response—that is, the opening of the door—but also to make clear to those intruded upon whom they were dealing with, to demonstrate strength, decisiveness, and power, to persuade those inside that all was lost, that they could only succumb, surrender, and relinquish all hope. This kind of knocking, commencing at once, with no preliminaries, in *forte* or outright *fortissimo,* was the equivalent of pounding—

and could be the first stage of forcing open the door in the event there was no response.

As I write of knocking, I am thinking of the world of sounds that ensconced Jews during the black seasons. One could say there are sounds characteristic of executioners. I'm not even thinking of the cracking of boots on the pavement, announcing that units were heading to the ghetto to drive people to Umschlagplatz. The cracking, like the marching songs they shouted out, was ominous. I'm thinking rather of sounds neutral in and of themselves, sounds ordinarily not connected to anything in particular or associated with fear. When I was hiding in the village with my mother, the hum of an approaching car elicited an intense, nearly unfathomable fear. In some sense this was unambiguous: cars passed by only rarely and belonged exclusively to Germans. When one appeared on that pitiful, out-of-the-way road, it portended nothing good. The sound of an engine could be the harbinger of death. To this day I remember my hellish terror when once it seemed to me that the hum had suddenly broken off, that the German car had stopped in front of the house where we could be found. That feeling—as if a rope were being tightened around my neck—still lives in me, as does the moment of relief when there was no longer any doubt that the car had continued on its way, that the Germans had not come to take us off to be killed or to murder us where we were.

It is not for their own sake that I am evoking the sounds of the occupation which, if they were to be arranged in some musical totality, would regardless of the volume comprise an infernal composition. I'm writing of them rather in order to tell of a certain event. My mother and I were hiding then at the Wolskis', occupying a corner of the kitchen in their small apartment. Up until a certain moment, things were relatively calm; still I feared everything, including going out beyond the courtyard, although it was summer and the neighboring fields and meadows might have seemed enticing. Not very far away, in one of the nearby villages, my father was hiding, and it was at dawn on just one of those summer days when we heard a delicate knocking on the kitchen window. It seems to me that at first my mother decided not to react, thinking perhaps that at so early an hour someone must have pressing business for our landlords, and that it was not for her to respond. After a while the knocking began again; perhaps she heard a whisper and wanted to see discreetly what was going on. She saw something she had not anticipated: standing before the window was my father. She was certain something had suddenly forced him to flee the place where he had been hiding.

Długi had found a hiding place for him with a certain middle-aged peasant. His cottage stood somewhere out of the way; having been widowed several years earlier, the peasant now lived there alone, his children dispersed throughout the surrounding area. He possessed only a small patch of land, and so had few obligations and could not complain of a lack of time. The time he had, he filled with drinking. It was difficult to come upon a moment when he was entirely sober. This was trying for my father, but in the beginning their relations were relatively proper. This peasant, whose name I can't remember, rented my father a corner in his crumbling homestead. The peasant was probably content, as he received some money (although not very much), he had someone to talk to, and—and this in my father's account was particularly important to him—he had an audience for his drunken monologues. After a while, the peasant became aware that, in 1943, keeping a Jew in his farmhouse exposed him to grave danger, and he demanded more money. It did not end there, though. In his mind there developed what was—one must admit objectively—an entirely rational idea. He announced to my father that, as a Jew, my father would surely be killed anyway, but it would not be good if the peasant, too, had to suffer or even die. Yet the consequence of such an illusionless view of reality was not to refuse my father permission to stay there. The peasant's conception went further. He informed my father that it would make no sense if my father were to perish in a simple and ordinary way, given that he had to be killed anyway. The best thing would be if the peasant himself were to take my father to the Germans, and in particular to the nearest gendarme outpost.

Certainly they would murder my father, but nothing would happen to the peasant himself, and moreover he would earn some money, because the Germans would give him a reward.

My father no doubt appreciated the rationality of this well-conceived arrangement, perhaps even admired the pragmatic intellect of his landlord, whose chattering he had hitherto treated only as drunken raving. Yet this bizarre proposition soon began to repeat itself obsessively—it became the central motif of candid evening talks—and my father grew aware that this was not merely meaningless babble flowing from successive bottles of moonshine. He no longer doubted that the situation was becoming serious, and graver with each passing day. It was difficult to persuade the author of such an idea—so lucid and well situated in reality, so fully considerate of the state of affairs under the occupation—that he should relinquish it. It was difficult to persuade him to expel from his alcohol-clouded head what had gestated therein. He was deaf to all arguments—they quite simply did not reach him, he was unable to part with his idea.

My father grew more certain with each passing day that this was not idle talk, and that he was increasingly at risk. Yet in spite of everything, he remained, as he had no other place to hide. He decided to flee only when this peasant, who remains anonymous to me, declared he'd had enough of all this. If my father did not allow the peasant to denounce my father to the Germans, then tomorrow the peasant would lead the Germans to the house, because it was time to get it over with already. This was, to be sure, a less ideal solution, since he would receive a smaller reward, but even so, he was sure to get something. The threat was delivered. For the first time, a concrete date had materialized. My father no longer had any illusions, nor any choice. He had to escape, even though it would be escaping into a void. He packed his few things, and by night slipped away from the cottage whose owner, even when impaired by alcohol, had such logical ideas.

Years later, my father told me that he'd had no exact plans. He understood that he could not stay there any longer, but he didn't know what he would do. He wanted to see us, to say goodbye, perhaps forever, for then every moment was felt to be the last. The uncertainty of the time defined all thoughts and actions without exception, and this held with particular force when something had changed and new factors had emerged, new factors, as a rule, meaning a new series of menaces. And at one such moment, my father knocked on the window of the kitchen in the corner of which we had nested. My mother realized at once that something had taken place that wasn't good. She didn't know what exactly, because while my parents were not living far from one another at the time, they were not in direct contact—such were the rules of an underground existence; if they did communicate any news or signs of life to each other, it was by way of Długi, who was always ready to rush forward with all kinds of valuable services. And so they faced the necessity of deciding what to do next. This stage in my father's wanderings had come decisively to an end. There was no longer any place for him in that area, something new had to be sought. At that time, "what next?" was among the most dramatic of questions, at various moments requiring an immediate answer, even when there was no good answer and each answer could be calamitous—and final. Sometimes there were, in essence, no answers. Sometimes things had played out in such a way that one could reasonably conclude all possibilities had exhausted themselves and there was no longer even the vaguest shadow of hope. Chance alone could decide a person's subsequent fate.

On this occasion it soon emerged that my father's situation was not yet so desperate, at least not with respect to the next few days. The Wolskis hurried forward with assistance, allowing my father to stay in their garden plot until some solution emerged. The plot was located not far from the railway tracks, a certain distance from the house where I was staying with my mother. There were some fruit trees growing there, and a vegetable garden that Pani Wolska tended. The plot was small. Nothing had been built there, save for a small wooden shed meant to accommodate not a person, but rather shovels, rakes, and other basic gardening tools. It was in this shed that my father was to hide. Within a short time he went there and stayed for a week, perhaps ten days. During that time someone brought him food, delivering it in such a way that no one would notice the unfamiliar man living on the garden plot and no one's interest—and more critically, no one's suspicions—would be aroused. One never knew whose eyes might reveal themselves to be the eyes of an informer.

My father's stay in the garden tool shed only briefly postponed the fundamental question: what next? In the end the need remained for a decision. My father decided that he would go to Warsaw. He knew his cousin's address and would go to her— perhaps she and her husband could help, advise, somehow point to some solution. Several, or perhaps more than a dozen, years before the war, this cousin of his had married a Catholic—or rather, as people said during the time of the occupation, an Aryan—to the whole family's astonishment (and surely to the dismay of the family's older and more conservative members), as mixed marriages were a rarity at that time. She did not go to the ghetto. Together with her husband, she moved to another apartment and suspended her dental practice. Both the cousin and her husband were involved in rescuing family members, thanks to which the cousin's sister survived the war together with her husband, who spoke Polish with an appalling accent—that terrible Yiddish intonation that was so difficult to unlearn and would have exposed him at once. For a long time he was forced to feign muteness.

My father learned that in Kielce his sister was living on the Aryan Side with her husband and daughter, who was my age. They were living under a fictitious name and were employed somewhere, and thus did my father decide to go to Kielce and find work. He remained for a long while in that city. He was employed as a worker at a company on the outskirts of town, and naturally he had false papers. Perhaps he would have lived to see the end of the war there, had he not been caught during a round-up and transported to a labor camp in Germany. He was not exposed as a Jew, and a series of miracles brought about his survival—but that is another story. Even in the most difficult circumstances dealt him by fate, it can be said that during the Holocaust his fortune was a good one.

As for the peasant who in the course of evening conversations revealed his intentions with truly drunken candor—he disappeared entirely. I don't know how his fate played out. I would think there would be nothing to evoke particular interest. He drank, and drank, until he drank himself to death. I confess, though, I would be gratified to know how he reacted that morning when he saw that the Jew—whose death was to improve his modest finances, if only by bringing in some insignificant sum for the next bottle—had disappeared. I suspect he prescribed an extra dose of moonshine for himself on that day.

✤

The Villa on Odolańska Street

When, more than a dozen years after the war, we decided to move from Pruszków to Warsaw, my mother categorically refused to agree to a new apartment either in the area that was once the ghetto or in Mokotów. The former was seemingly self-evident: it's difficult to live an ordinary, everyday life on a piece of land where the most hideous things took place, where one lived through the most hellish experiences, where the soil is saturated with depravity and anguish to an extent possible only on killing fields, or in places of mass murder. There is no way to live a calm—even if vaguely normal—life in a cemetery, even if there are no literal graves. It's not possible to settle permanently in places where every stone, every name, every architectural detail can become a reminder, for nothing is neutral and devoid of meaning, even in a ruined city deliberately and thoroughly leveled to the ground.

Her resistance to Mokotów, though, seemed curious, for nothing connected either my mother or the family to that neighborhood. In the beginning I didn't understand where her aversion came from, and only after some time did I realize that this, too, had its origin in those times, in a certain event that left lasting traces in my mother's consciousness—and in my memory. It happened on a certain street in Mokotów on a bleak day in December 1943. It was the result of an unusual chance occurrence that it was not our fate to hide in that part of the city.

We had arrived in Warsaw because we could no longer take
cover in R.; that village, together with the surrounding area, had
grown dangerous. We had nowhere to go, and a friend found us
a place for a short time with some people named Bobrowski on
Litewska Street—a short time, because it was contingent upon
steep payments and, moreover, for various reasons, it was particularly unsafe, hence staying there could only be a momentary solution. The Bobrowskis' apartment deserves description. It was
large, with many rooms, situated on the uppermost floor of an
elegant home on Litewska Street, and so bordering the German
district; before the war it had undoubtedly belonged to a wealthy
bourgeois family, its present tenants had moved there during the
occupation.

They were people of business, undoubtedly faring rather well.
They knew how to make a fortune from wartime. They were a
young couple without children; living with them was an older
(although not yet old) and unusually energetic woman whom
they called Mamusia. Whose mother she was, I don't know. They
were involved in trade; Mamusia, I think, even had a booth at
the Różycki bazaar, and Bobrowski—if I'm not mistaken—at
Kercelak (or vice versa). Pani Bobrowska assisted in their business endeavors, but most important, she was in charge of what
went on in the apartment—and much went on, as it was a kind
of hotel for Jews in hiding (naturally those whose identities were
appropriately concealed). Most of the rooms were rented to those
who—like my mother and me—were staying for only a short
time; one was occupied by permanent tenants: a man whom they
called—if I'm remembering correctly—the engineer, together
with his son and another boy who was there without his family.
Both of the boys were named Stefan, the engineer gave them lessons; once or twice I sat in on these, too. Pani Bobrowska, who
was not one reticent to talk, admitted to my mother that she was
allowing the forlorn Stefanek to stay there for only a small fee, because his family had formally committed to turning over to her
an enormous estate after the war. Everything here was a question
of money—sentiments played no role, although it should be

said that she treated the boy well. Naturally the Bobrowskis were aware that they had chosen a precarious means of amassing wealth. They must have realized that hiding Jews for profit exposed them to the death penalty no less than did hiding them out of friendship or other beneficent, humanitarian motives. They had taken some safety precautions, there were alcoves adequate for times when the Bobrowskis wished to conceal from guests and other visitors what was going on in the apartment, but these camouflaged places would have proven themselves ineffectual in the event of a German raid and search.

While we were staying in that apartment on Litewska Street, attempts were being made to find a longer-term hiding place. Procuring even the worst room for a Jewish woman with a child was, understandably, a nontrivial task. But this finally was achieved. A place was found! As usual, it was found with the help of the great and wonderful Irena Sendlerowa, the guardian angel of those in hiding. (Irena Sendlerowa brought about the rescue of as many as two and a half thousand Jewish children!) On one early morning in December we were to move to Mokotów, where we were to be settled in the basement of an inhabited though unfinished villa on Odolańska Street. I'm unable to say whether the owner realized from the beginning to whom she was renting the room for a small sum, if she was told this openly, or if she only guessed. But she agreed, and this was the most important thing. We were to appear at the arranged time, just after the curfew had ended.

And so it happened. For us, hunted and homeless, that basement in the villa on Odolańska Street became a tremendous prospect, even though there was, of course, no guarantee that it was a secure refuge. During those times, for those like us, there were no secure places; any refuge, at any given moment, could become the setting for a final tragedy. I understood this as well as my mother did, yet even so, in seeking a place to hide, we had to sustain hope that it would be a place where we might survive. With such hope we set out for Odolańska Street. And when we had already reached our destination, having moved through the streets in such a way as not to draw anyone's attention, we saw something we could not have anticipated, something that completely stunned us: a house destroyed by fire. During the occupation the adjective "burnt" had a particular meaning—it described a place that had been exposed, unmasked, a place where, for reasons of safety, it was no longer possible to hide or to engage in underground activity. In this case, however, the adjective was not a metaphorical one. We saw something we could not believe—a villa just after a fire had been put out, an ordinary, natural fire having nothing to do with the war and the occupation, a fire that might have broken out in peaceful and untroubled times. The fire brigade had only just left.

We found ourselves in a ruined building, which was a calamity for us as well. While the house had been burned to the ground, in the basement (as is frequently the case after a fire) there was ankle-deep water. We crouched in a corner, not knowing what to do. The owner of the villa had not waited for us. One needn't wonder that in such a situation she had forgotten about having arranged to meet us—doubtless she had forgotten about our existence entirely. I know nothing about her and am unable to describe her, yet before my eyes remains the figure of a tall, thin woman in a state of shock and terror, darting about something that just yesterday had been her home. There were still some people around, tenants perhaps, or acquaintances come to help the woman who had met with such great misfortune, or perhaps officials come to determine the cause of the fire or appraise the damages. I sat with my mother in the least visible corner, where there was relatively little water, and we tried to behave in such a way as to remain unnoticed, for we had no assurance that one of these people would not turn out to be an informer who would expose us. We sat, crushed by misfortune, defenseless and paralyzed by what had happened. My mother faced the necessity of deciding what to do, but she was clearly in no state to do this. After all, no possibilities even vaguely delineated themselves. Where were we to go? There were no positions, known to us or otherwise, to which we could retreat. We had come upon difficulties in contacting our family in Warsaw; my father was in Kielce at the time, employed as a laborer, there was no way to communicate with our Polish friends who had been helping us, I don't know if my mother remembered their phone numbers; for reasons of safety, she would not have written them down. In any case, if there had been a telephone in the ruined villa, it was undoubtedly no longer working after the disaster. We were left to our own fate, in some sense severed from the world.

And so we sat impassively in hunger and cold. My mother resolved that we would remain there until the following day, as we had nowhere to go; perhaps after the initial cleanup it would turn out that the basement we were to have lived in would be inhabitable despite everything. This might be our chance. So we sat idly and waited to see how things would play out. And suddenly the direction they were taking revealed itself. After we had spent several hours barely existing in the ruined basement, much of which was covered with water, the owner of the villa came for us. She didn't come, though, because she had only just remembered or noticed us; she had probably known the whole time that we were sitting in that corner of the flooded basement. She came to pass along important news or rather, in a sense, to pass along instructions. In this unusual, disastrous situation there were many different people moving about the house, and she told us that our presence had been observed. In particular we had drawn the attention of the new tenants who had moved in several days earlier. She didn't know who they were; they might be *Volksdeutsche*. What sort of people they were was unknown, it was not impossible that they would inform on us. The situation was becoming desperately unsafe, we had to abandon that burnt villa at once. She said this in an irrefutable, decisive voice that excluded the possibility of any further questions or discussion. It was unmistakably the case that she could not have acted otherwise. She was aware of the danger, and she acted on behalf of our own good as well, even though she was not able to help us, she herself had fallen victim to misfortune. And it was true that a moment before, my mother and I had been disconcerted by a young woman who had looked at us with distrusting inquisitiveness.

There was no doubt that the owner of the villa knew who we were. We had to fulfill her command at once, clearly it followed from a realistic assessment of the situation, and not from the fact—or not only from the fact—that she wanted to be rid of us as quickly as possible, as we could bring misfortune upon her as well. My mother must have been beset by terror still greater than that she had felt when she saw the burnt house. After a short while she made a decision: we would go back to the Bobrowskis. Of course we couldn't be certain they would take us in, but neither was there another solution. When we reached the door of the apartment on Litewska Street, my mother rang the bell softly. But would there even be any response? She rang again—and only after some time did Pani Bobrowska approach the door with the customary inquiry: who's there? Understandably, in an apartment where Jews were hiding, any instance of unarranged or unforeseen knocking necessarily inspired terror and apprehension and required a series of rapid undertakings if only to conceal what should not be noticed by even the most benign or sympathetic visitor. Quietly my mother said who she was and what had happened. The response was harsh words of refusal. New tenants had already arrived, and perhaps the Bobrowskis were also worried they would not receive payment. My mother repeated her request, now a plea, assuring Pani Bobrowska that even now, the bill would be taken care of, the stakes were at their highest: being left on the streets just before the curfew was an unambiguous death sentence. Pani Bobrowska declared that she and her husband "were not a charitable institution"—but in the end, she did open the door. The events of that awful day had come full circle: in the evening we returned to the place which that morning it had seemed we were abandoning forever.

My mother remained at the Bobrowskis for two, perhaps three, days. I stayed longer, perhaps a week. A position was quickly found for her as a maid for a certain woman, a teacher in Otwock; this, too, was through Pani Irena, who in the season of great dy-

ing devoted her entire life to saving Jews. This was my first separation from my mother, and I had to part with her for a long
time, until the end of the war. This came as a terrible shock, even
though my mother explained to me that we could no longer be
together. Of the time I spent alone at the Bobrowskis little has
stayed in my memory—only a domestic fight late one evening,
perhaps it was already night. I was an involuntary witness, since
it occurred in the room where they had put me. I pretended to
be sleeping, I acted as if I were not there, but I couldn't help but
hear the dreadful screams. The couple flung accusations at each
other—they accused each other of the most terrible things—and
every so often, the woman they called Mamusia would intervene
in the argument, first on one side, then on the other, or then again
as mediator. The scene stopped just short of violence; the tall
and imposing Pani Bobrowska would certainly have fought ably
against her diminutive and scrawny spouse, who stood just above
her shoulder (or so my memory has preserved them—whether
this corresponds to how they actually looked, I can't be sure). The
following day I left the apartment on Litewska Street. A new
chapter in my life in hiding was about to begin.

And here I could close the narrative of this episode of my history during the occupation. I feel, though, the need to add something further, for I wonder if that fire at the villa on Odolańska
Street—which to both me and my mother seemed such a disastrous misfortune—was not the accident to which we owe our
lives. Had we stayed in that basement for even a short time, those
new tenants, whom the owner barely knew and who might have
been *Volksdeutsche,* would undoubtedly have taken an interest in
us. Of course it's impossible to know where that interest would
have led, perhaps to denunciation and execution. For Jews in hiding, anyone not absolutely trusted, any stranger or passerby was
a potential executioner. So, too, could that young woman gazing
at us with a piercing glance have been an executioner, even
though the possibility is not to be excluded that her gaze was one
of natural female curiosity. So now, when from such a great distance I tell of the events of a certain December day in 1943, I

wonder whether that fire on Odolańska Street was not a fortunate misfortune, and whether if not for that fire, my mother and
I would have managed to survive the occupation. Perhaps the
owner of the villa also owes her life to that fire, since the Germans would have unquestionably condemned her to death for
hiding Jews in her home.

When I think now about my time in hiding on the Aryan
Side, about the flight from death, I'm overwhelmed by the great
role played by chance—chance that was auspicious or at times
seemingly auspicious or seemingly inauspicious, chance deciding survival or extinction, chance deciding life or death, chance
sudden and not only unforeseen (such is always the case), but also
bewildering, irrational, and contrary to all rules of probability,
chance that was all the more incalculable for materializing in a
world governed by draconian determinism—after all, one did
not decide for oneself whether or not one was a Jew. So often it
was precisely chance that determined life or death. It weighed
upon human fate to a much greater degree than in calmer times,
when determinisms did not operate with such forcefulness.

The House beneath the Eagles

My stay with the Felicjanka nuns lasted a short time, probably no more than two weeks; it quickly emerged that I could stay there no longer. I had just turned nine, and the Otwock orphanage housed children up to age seven. I was placed in the oldest group, but even so I was taller than my peers, which drew attention. The fundamental principle of being in hiding was to avoid precisely this, and rather to blend into the crowd, to become someone without qualities, the most ordinary of the ordinary. In this case such a course turned out to be unfeasible, and I had to abandon that refuge. Very little has remained in my memory from that short and comparatively undramatic episode—only that the building housing the orphanage was made of wood, that it seemed to me to be large, and that the nuns wore brown habits and veils. And that the sister who looked after the older group had a beautiful, intriguing name: Prudencja. Of course I didn't know what this meant in Latin and as this was my first experience in a convent, I also didn't know that the names taken by nuns often depart from the names one encounters in the secular world.

I do, though, remember a certain event, in and of itself minor and of little significance. It, too, might have faded from my memory had I not, considerably later, after the war, learned what was hidden behind it, and thus what an unusual dimension it possessed. It was fortunate that, at the time, I realized nothing,

and so was able to behave normally, to be one—albeit one dis-
concertingly tall—among a crowd of children. One day Sister
Prudencja informed us that we would be going on an outing to
visit a certain esteemed and pious lady, a teacher who was a patron of our orphanage. Today it's difficult for me to discern that
visit's specific objective—perhaps it was only to divert the children from the monotony of those winter days, which failed to
differentiate themselves in any way one from the other. The visit
constituted an undoubted attraction, if only because it was something new. Sister Prudencja arranged us into either pairs or groups
of four, and we set out.

This good lady's home was, I imagine, not far away, I remember clearly that it was located on a spacious, fenced-in plot
of land; the children quickly ran off in search of the remaining
snow so as to make snowballs. It was a good-sized wooden villa,
most likely in Zakopane style, one of the many built around the
capital at the beginning of the twentieth century. After some
time had passed we were invited inside, and we found ourselves
in a large, rather dark room, which must have served as a salon.
The lady of the house told us something uplifting and gave us
each a piece of candy. What fixed itself in my memory most
vividly, though, were not these unimportant events, but the
room itself or rather one element of that room: namely, two, perhaps even three, stuffed birds, eagles, as we were shortly to learn.
They were secured in opposite corners of the room beneath the
ceiling, secured in an extremely peculiar position, leaning as if
they were about to break into flight and attack someone. My attention was riveted on their sharp beaks. Never had I seen anything like this. I was astonished that dead birds could serve as
decoration. Before the war I had been to the zoo, but there were
no such monstrous things there, and of the birds, it had been the
noisy and colorful parrots that had enchanted me.

After the visit, which lasted an hour and a half, perhaps two
hours, we returned to the orphanage. So concluded this minor
event, or thus it seemed to me at the time. Nothing occurred,
and so why tell of it? And yet, given what I learned from my

mother many years later, the tale is worth telling. For in that very house, for that very woman who entertained the children from the Felicjanka nuns' orphanage that day, my mother was working as a maid. She was aware that I, too, was in Otwock (although I didn't know she was there), but she wasn't permitted to have any contact with me. I had been taken in as an orphan, and my mother had false papers, according to which she was unmarried. Naturally anything that might expose these fictions could have fatal consequences, and thus anything that might cast these stories into doubt was categorically forbidden. My mother understood this perfectly—she knew she couldn't violate the rules of being in hiding—yet she hadn't anticipated that in the house where she lived and worked as a maid she would see me, and so she found herself in a particularly trying situation, one requiring a certain kind of behavior. She had to concentrate all her efforts to ensure that I wouldn't notice her, for she might, reasonably, have expected that my reaction would be spontaneous, emotional, reckless. By that time I had internalized the basic rules of being in hiding, yet if faced with such a test, I undoubtedly would not have passed, especially so soon after I'd been separated from my mother. Only a short time before I could not have even imagined my life apart from her, yet it quickly came about that I was forced to adapt to the new situation and to exist in a sea of strangeness.

My mother told me not only of that unusual winter day, but also of the house adorned with stuffed eagles, of what happened there, and above all of the woman she worked for, Pani B. My mother disliked returning to the time of the occupation, she avoided reminiscing, yet what she did disclose to me of her experiences during that time was so moving and penetrating, so precise and saturated with details, that I remember all of it to this day. I unexpectedly wandered upon a reference to that house and that woman in Helena Szereszewska's memoirs *The Cross and the Mezuzah;* her nephew, a young boy named Józio (Pani B. appears in these memoirs under a slightly different name, perhaps because the author's memory deceived her), was hidden in Pani

B.'s home. "He is taken care of mostly by the maid, Walerka. But what came to light? That this maid is a Jewess, the sister of Henryk Szpilfogel's wife." Henryk Szpilfogel's wife was my aunt Maria, and her sister was my mother. She did not go by the name of Walerka, though—she was Panna Zofia.

My mother remembered Józio well, he was not much older than I was. He survived the war and left for Israel, where he became a well-regarded architect, in addition to his work in archaeology. He died not long ago, after a sudden and serious illness. She also recalled a certain attorney who hid for a time in the recesses of Pani B.'s spacious home; my mother knew him from the ghetto, and when circumstances allowed, she would exchange a few words with him. Many other things were going on as well in that house where Jews were hiding. Every so often there would be meetings of resistance activists; my mother quickly came to understand that these were important figures in the Otwock underground. Pani B. had employed my mother not only because it cost so little, but also because my mother had come with good references, recommended by Pani Irena, and thus could be trusted. This trust was evinced by, among other things, the fact that Pani B. would give my mother the Home Army's "Information Bulletin" to read. This was of enormous significance to my mother because from the bulletin she learned what was happening, it also drew her into another world, serving as psychological support.

Did Pani B. realize that my mother was a Jewess? In all likelihood Pani B. was never told openly, yet after all, she could not but have guessed, all the more so given that, notwithstanding her efforts to perform her domestic duties as well as possible, the new girl Friday's speech and behavior departed from that of the typical servant—moreover my mother was completely alone in an unfamiliar, alien world, tossed to Otwock by fate and directed to the villa beneath the eagles. I think Pani B. chose not to know of my mother's origins, she left the matter in suspension, preferring not to reflect upon it, she was satisfied with my mother's work, so Panna Zofia was to be simply Panna Zofia. And this, too, speaks well of Pani B.

My mother spoke appreciatively of Pani B.'s merits and virtues, and emphasized her courage and devotion to the cause, yet at the same time she did not conceal that this was only one side of Pani B.'s personality. For that energetic, resourceful woman who rushed forward to help those in need was a household tyrant with a corporal's soul who tolerated not even the vaguest sign of opposition or the minutest trace of autonomy; she was the kind of despot who interpreted the slightest gesture in any way displeasing to her as a sign of rebellion, necessary beyond a shadow of a doubt to suppress at once by any possible means. And in no way did this pertain only to Panna Zofia, who in the end was just a maid, admittedly working for nothing, for no money, but rather only for a bare subsistence and a corner to sleep in, who was content to have found a safe refuge, and aware that she must acquiesce to everything in order not to lose it. This held true as well for Pani B.'s three stepdaughters, the oldest around twenty, the other two slightly younger.

Pani B. married late, at an age when in those times she would have been labeled an old maid. She married a widower who brought as a dowry not only the house with the salon adorned with stuffed eagles, but also three daughters from his first marriage. Pani B. had no children of her own, but now had to take charge of raising the young ladies. Her husband died fairly soon thereafter, at the very beginning of the war or perhaps even before, leaving Pani B. with the three girls. It's not impossible that she hated them, that their very existence irritated her—and that she behaved according to the paradigm of the cruel, evil stepmother known from numerous fairy tales. Perhaps, though, the issue was not that they were stepdaughters. Perhaps Pani B. would have acted similarly toward anyone who was dependent upon her in any way. Her authoritarian personality manifested itself toward family and friends as well as vague acquaintances; in every situation, she determined to impose her own will, and she destroyed everything that could be a potential obstacle. According to my mother's account, those three young girls became slaves, victims of terror. Pani B. refused to acknowledge the possibility that their behavior could take a form other than that of unconditional obedience. She acted as if her primary goal were the destruction of their personalities, as if she desired to reduce them to the status of passive and uncritical executrices of her instructions and demands. Not only attempts at resistance, but even instances of reluctance met with sharp counterattacks, reprimands, and punishments. A ceaseless *psychomachia* went on in that villa. It was in essence a civil war, largely independent of the one that proceeded relentlessly in the surrounding world.

My mother tried to act as if this conflict did not exist, or at least as if she did not notice it. Yet she understood well what was going on, and she empathized with the three ill-treated girls. Years later, when these matters belonged to an irretrievably bygone past, she recalled these girls warmly and with sympathy. After all, she too was subjected to the same treatment as were they, the scope of Pani B.'s military discipline was universal, the nature of that home rested on it. She granted herself absolute authority in every matter with respect to everyone, even the stinginess taken to caricatured proportions served the regime. My mother felt that she was treated like a dirty rag, and not because in the unusual conditions of the occupation it had befallen her to become a maid. She understood the specificity of these conditions and that her life was at stake. She performed her duties well, not only because she was conscientious by nature, but also—and perhaps most important—because she was dependent upon this position. It provided her with a chance of survival. And she was admonished for everything: for a speck of dust found on the floor, for a sugar bowl standing an inch away from the spot where—in Pani B.'s opinion—it ought to be. My mother not only had to remember all of Pani B.'s injunctions and prohibitions, but she also had to anticipate precisely what Pani B. would desire at a certain moment, and the moods and caprices of this Tsaritsa Catherine the Great within the contours of an Otwock home were not always easy to surmise. Pani B.'s forceful personality made itself felt even in the intonation with which she addressed members of her household. Her very manner of speaking was to effect not only their subordination to her and the exclusion of any possibility of opposition, but also their paralysis and reduction to the status of objects, to things like tables or chairs that could be moved at will. Pani B.'s manner of speaking expressed what could be called the surety of dominance that characterizes absolute monarchs, yet at once it also conveyed the disgust Pani B. harbored toward the women dependent on her. She acted as if her primary objective were their humiliation.

Of the many psychological wounds my mother took away from the occupation, those connected with her stay in that house were among the most severe. They lasted for a long time, until the end of her life. Humiliations are absorbed especially deeply, they resist being forgotten—and this is true regardless of the circumstances, and thus also true when one realizes that submitting to this kind of psychologically destructive treatment is a price that must be paid because there is no other choice. When telling years later of Pani B.'s despotism, of her distinctively dreadful character, my mother did not deny her merits and virtues, her courage, energy, and dedication. Rather it intrigued my mother how such disparate elements could have coexisted in one woman, how such contradictions could have taken shape in her, even if they did not form a harmonious whole (which no doubt they did not). Years later this question intrigues me as well: how did it come about that someone who was a tyrant at home, who destroyed everyone who was in any way dependent on her, acted so nobly and courageously in her public life?

By the time I, together with the group of children led by Sister Prudencja, unexpectedly appeared in my mother's sphere of vision, my mother already knew much about Pani B.'s conduct and personality. Even though she had only just begun to work for her, my mother understood well Pani B.'s unequivocal beliefs, and this, too, bore on her behavior on that unusual day when she suddenly saw her own child. My mother understood that she could not expose herself, that this would threaten her with dismissal from her job—not even because Pani B. would have then ascertained beyond any doubt that my mother was a Jewess. The issue lay in something else. My mother, like the majority of refugees from the camps and ghettos in hiding, had false papers, according to which—as I've mentioned—she was not married. For Pani B., a situation wherein an unmarried woman was revealed as having a child would be morally unacceptable, even were she to realize that this was a fiction necessary for existence on the Aryan Side. Pani B. was a person of principle, and her ethical code did not foresee cases of this kind, she would not have been able to keep so immoral a person in her home. My mother had no doubts about this, and for this reason, too, she was especially cautious. That day was uniquely trying for her. After all, she wanted to come to me, yet had to conceal herself from me, and at the same time had to take care that her behavior did not seem odd or incomprehensible to anyone around her.

On that ordinary January day I was unaware of these complications. I don't remember what Pani B. looked like, although I must have seen her since she gave me, like all of the children, a piece of candy. She did not pique my interest. After all, I didn't know that my mother's fate depended on her. I was intrigued by the stuffed birds with powerful beaks and sharp claws, fixed in poses I found bizarre, perched as if they were about to attack anyone who appeared in that room. To this day I can see them.

※

A Quarter Hour Passed in a Pastry Shop

I spent little more than ten days among the nuns in Czersk. As the course of events was to reveal, I'd been placed there without their having been informed about my origins, and so I found myself in the role of the cuckoo's egg, tossed into the nest without the knowledge and consent of its owner. Once the nuns came to understand who I was, they did not let me stay. A few years ago I was reminded of that short visit, undistinguished by anything in particular, while reading a book about convents that rescued Jewish children. One of the nuns who ran that small orphanage claimed they'd hidden there a large number of Jewish children, refusing only once, in fear of having too many, which naturally increased the danger. The rejection fell upon a certain boy, for they knew members of his family were still alive and he would not be left on his own. I'm nearly certain she was speaking of me, for I don't suppose in that time and place something identical could have befallen one of my contemporaries. I happened upon the pages of that book, stunned that after several decades anyone apart from myself possessed a memory of that event.

It was Maria, my mother's younger sister, who took me to Warsaw, as among all the family members in hiding, it was she who moved about on the Aryan Side most freely. She possessed what were then called "good looks," which were not merely a privilege, but moreover a divine bestowal. Good looks meant that the person in hiding aroused less suspicion. People with good looks did not draw attention, they could blend into the crowd, it was easier for them to play the role of someone they were not. Maria's looks were exquisite; she was an attractive blond who looked as if she had been born into a noble estate, rather than into a Jewish merchant's family. Anyone with less than intimate knowledge would never have discerned what origins lay hidden behind her impeccable Slavic beauty. And so when I'd again found myself homeless and no one knew what to do with me, it fell to Maria to deal with my very problematic situation. She lived as a subtenant in a room with her daughter, who was four years younger than I, but couldn't take me there for fear of rousing suspicions. There was a desperate search for a place for even one or two nights, until a longer-term solution could be found. I'm unable to trace the chronology of my miserable roamings on the Aryan Side or to situate events on a time line with any precision, and so I'm not certain if it was then or earlier that I stayed for a few days with a couple living in Ochota. Unfortunately I don't know their names—I didn't then, either— but I've preserved that family in my memory with gratitude. Suddenly I'd found myself in another reality, in a home that was warm and pleasant, where everyone was welcoming to me, the older people as well as the younger ones, as there were also two almost-grown children—an eighteen-year-old who attended school but in reality was involved in the underground (he spoke of these experiences to his parents, seeming not to take my presence into consideration, as of course a child understands nothing!), as well as a girl a bit younger, and it was mainly she who took care of me.

This idyllic interlude was brief. On the day in question a place was being sought for me; I think it was just then, thanks to the assistance of the wonderful and irreplaceable Irena Sendlerowa, that my trip to Turkowice was arranged. I was walking through the city with Maria, I'm unable to reconstruct our path, I know only that these events took place downtown. Neither can I name the concrete goal of our roaming, for during those times one did not go out unless it was of the utmost necessity. I remember one short episode, lasting not more than a quarter hour, but a story I believe to be worth telling after all these years.

Maria had to make a phone call. We entered a small pastry shop where she thought there was a telephone. As it turned out, there was not. Faced with this situation, Maria decided to leave me there alone for a few minutes, she bought me a pastry, choosing the least visible table in a fairly dark corner, and told me she would be back right away, as soon as she had made the phone call. She told the same thing to the woman who had served us, who must have been the shop owner. There were no more than five tables and very few people, I could hear everything. In the beginning, it seemed to me that all was calm, and I sat very quietly, like a mouse hiding beneath a broomstick, waiting as I'd been told to—and fortunately, nothing was happening. I ate my pastry, and what the women (there were no men) were chatting about among themselves didn't concern me. Yet after a while I couldn't escape the realization that the scene was playing out otherwise. It was difficult to harbor any doubts that I had become the center of attention. The women—perhaps shop assistants, perhaps customers—had gathered around the shop owner, whispering and observing me intently. By this time I was a sufficiently experienced Jewish child in hiding to understand at once what this meant and what it could foreshadow. My level of fear heightened radically.

I felt their observation of me palpably, as if I had been struck. The women stared at me as if I were an extraordinary monster, whose very existence called into question the laws of nature, and as if they would have to decide what to do with me that very moment, for things could not remain as they were. Fragments of their conversation reached me that were sufficiently telling. I was not experiencing delusions, they were talking about me. As usual in such situations, I would have most preferred to melt into the ground. I heard "A Jew, there's no question, a Jew." "She certainly isn't, but him—he's a Jew." "She's foisted him off onto us." The women deliberated: what should they do with me? The shop owner opened the door leading to the back room where the oven must have been, and called out "Hela! Hela, come look." And after some time Hela appeared in a flour-covered apron, obviously interrupted from her work. The women awaited her judgment; clearly they valued her opinion. Perhaps she was an authority on various matters, or even an expert in racial questions, within the context of the pastry shop, which for me had ceased to be a calm and peaceful space. One more pair of piercing eyes came forward to examine me.

I tried not to think of how it would end. I sank into myself. I reached a state that can descend amid all-consuming fear, a state of its own kind of indifference and internal paralysis, difficult to comprehend, and yet explicable in the sense that at such moments, a person—even a child, as I was at the time—is conscious of having no influence over his own fate, of rather coming in some sense to resemble an object. There was no escape from the understanding that my situation was worsening from moment to moment. No longer were the women content to observe me from afar, to establish my origins collectively from a distance. Perhaps they wanted confirmation, some final justification for the decision they would reach (and quite possibly already had reached). I heard one of them say, "We have to let the police know."

The women, having discussed the matter and their curiosity now piqued, came nearer; they approached the table where I sat. So began the interrogation. First one of them asked my name. I had false papers, I'd learned my identity, and I answered politely. Another was curious about my relationship to the woman who'd brought me there. I answered again, this time truthfully. Later I would learn that the next stage in this type of examination was generally the demand to recite one of the most common prayers—a very good test, as it enabled the examiner to tell at once a Catholic from a non-Catholic, a Pole from a non-Pole. However, the women bypassed this stage, perhaps because they were inexperienced. They continued to inundate me with questions: What were my parents doing? Where was I from? Where had I recently been? Where was I going? . . . and so forth. They tried to pose their questions gently, at times even sweetly, but I was not deceived by their tone, it required no great perspicacity to sense that behind this gentle tone lurked fury and aggression. They spoke to me as to a child, and yet at once as to a defendant or even an acknowledged criminal. Now that years have passed, I don't believe they were driven by pure hatred or resentment; rather, they dreaded the problem that had suddenly fallen into their laps and were prepared to do anything—by whatever means and at whatever price—to rid themselves of it as quickly as possible. And ridding themselves of the problem, I knew, meant ridding themselves of me.

The women put to me various questions, which by then I'd ceased to answer, only from time to time muttering a "yes" or "no." Many of the questions I wouldn't have been able to answer, others I was afraid to answer, even if only so as to avoid entrapping myself, to avoid invoking conflicting facts and thereby giving myself away completely. Yet I heard not only the questions directed at me, but also the comments the women expressed more quietly, to the side, as if only to themselves, but in such a way that I couldn't fail to hear. Most often they spit out the threatening word "Jew," but also, most terrifyingly, they kept repeating, "We have to let the police know." I was aware that this was the equivalent of a death sentence. If I'd then known something about Mediterranean mythology, I would doubtlessly have thought I'd landed in the possession of the Erinyes, the Furies, desirous of mutilating me. Yet would such an analogy be appropriate? For those women were not possessed by an uncontrollable hatred. They weren't breathing the fire of lust for vengeance; they had nothing for which to avenge themselves on me. These were normal, ordinary women, in their own way decent and resourceful, hardworking, undoubtedly scrambling to take care of their families in the difficult conditions of the occupation. Neither would I exclude the possibility that they were exemplary wives and mothers, perhaps religious, possessing a whole array of virtues. They had found themselves in a situation that felt to them trying and threatening, and they wished to confront it directly. They only did not think at what price. Perhaps this transcended their imaginations—although they must have known how it would end if they were to "let them know"—or perhaps such thoughts were simply not within the boundaries of moral reflection accessible to them.

After about a quarter hour, Maria returned, having been gone a bit longer than she'd supposed, as she'd had difficulty finding a telephone. Her return was my salvation, and I think that a stone fell from the women's hearts as well—their problem disappeared. When Maria saw a circle of people gathered around my table, she understood at once what was going on. She took me by the hand and we left as quickly as possible. I'd escaped intact.

✻

Jasio the Redhead

I knew who I was, I never forgot, I thought constantly of implications arising from this fact; yet I never knew nor wanted to know who others were. I simply didn't think about whether those around me were similar to myself, whether, like me, they were condemned to the worst. This question lay outside the scope of my reflection; in general I tried to act as if I were the only one in such a situation. Only several decades later did I learn that the nuns in Turkowice had hidden and rescued over thirty Jewish children—a very large, an improbably large, number, every seventh or eighth child there was marked by origins that, if revealed, equated to a death sentence. At times, however, it became impossible not to think about this, as when someone committed an indiscretion and said something that exposed himself.

On one occasion a certain boy my own age, or only a bit younger, told of having an eccentric aunt who, at a certain moment, began to go to church but didn't know how to behave there and so would make various mistakes during the services or do things that were obviously inappropriate. I grasped at once what was going on and thought: what an imbecile—he's letting his classmates know that this eccentric aunt is a Jew, and thus that he, too, given that he has such an aunt, is a Jew. I never would have told of anything that could have so exposed me, an internal warning system was already enabled, and it turned itself on instantaneously whenever something so much as crept to the edge of my tongue that might have—even indirectly—testified to my origins. I was well aware of, and had deeply internalized, the rules of hiding, and I took care not to depart from them. Yet there were occasions when something I couldn't have foreseen worked against me. Until I left the ghetto, I had spent my time almost exclusively among adults, and thus had assimilated words my Turkowice classmates didn't know, words they found incomprehensible and suspicious. Once I used the word "archipelago." It sounded strange to them, and one of the boys claimed that everything foreign-sounding was Jewish, and declared, "He's a Jew, because he speaks Yiddish." From that moment on, I was careful not to use words that could evoke my classmates' suspicion, even though I was perfectly well aware that such words had nothing in common with Yiddish. In any case, I quickly forgot them, and my vocabulary become just as basic as the others'.

I mention this to recall the case of one boy, a case that was entirely different, because everyone knew that he was Jewish. He became fixed in my memory as Jasio the Redhead. I think this is what he was called, although I can't be sure that my memory is entirely trustworthy. One thing is certain: all that is important in this dismal story fully corresponds to the facts and is entirely free of invention. What his name was, I don't know. When he appeared in Turkowice he must have borne a Jewish name and surname, but the nuns made efforts to secure false papers for him so that, like the others in hiding, he would have a Polish name; this was the first condition that had to be fulfilled when attempting to rescue someone. In the event of a German inspection, at least the papers should be in order.

Jasio the Redhead appeared in Turkowice several months before I did, he was alone, no one had brought him. He appeared starved, in a state of extreme exhaustion, hovering, it was said, between life and death. He told them who he was and asked for help. He was around fourteen and had a long history. He had come from Lwów and had lost his whole family during the liquidation of the ghetto there; he had miraculously managed to evade death—I don't know in what way. He knew no one he could ask for help, and set off into the world in hope of finding a means of survival outside of his own hometown. He went from village to village, from forest to forest, stopping where he could, leading the life of an animal fleeing from hunters. He begged the local peasants for food, and some fed him, while others chased him away. He came a long way given that in his flight from extermination he made it from Lwów to the vicinity of Hrubieszów. When he had already reached the edge of his strength, someone advised him to head toward Turkowice, for the kind nuns there would surely take care of him. And that came to pass. He didn't conceal who he was—this would have served no purpose in any event, as it was difficult for a hunted Jewish boy to hide anything, all was immediately apparent. There was not even so much as a moment's vacillation. Mother Superior, the good spirit of Turkowice, at once decided to take in the unexpected new arrival, even though she must have realized that doing so was doubly unsafe: he had appeared unconcealed, not among Polish children, but as a wandering Jew who had no chance of disguising or even camouflaging his origins in any way. And the news quickly spread: a Jewish boy had come and been taken in.

What I have told of up to this point belongs, from my perspective, to prehistory, because it occurred at a time when I was not yet in Turkowice, although it must have been spoken of quite a lot insofar as I've remembered events I didn't myself witness. Jasio the Redhead inscribed himself in my memory not only because his story was widely known, but also because he stood out—he distinguished himself by attributes particularly disadvantageous in a world where one of the conditions for survival was imitation. It was critical to resemble the surroundings as much as possible, to be inconspicuous, unnoticed, one among many, and Jasio the Redhead was not inconspicuous, the very redness of his hair was impossible not to notice, this itself drew attention to him. He also spoke a bit differently than the people of Turkowice. I'm not referring to Yiddish accretions, because if these did emerge, they were easily gotten rid of, if only by mimicry. The style of speech in Turkowice was a bit singsong and drawn out, but he did this with much more intensity, the way people spoke in Lwów and the eastern borderlands, and so his pronunciation, too, drew attention to him.

I remember him even though he was in another group, unless I am mistaken, the group looked after by Sister Józefa. He set himself apart in still another way: he was extremely energetic and outgoing. All knew him and to some extent approved of him, which was stranger still (and worthy of emphasis) given that many of the boys were not sympathetic toward Jews—they had clearly absorbed the images and judgments disseminated by racist propaganda—and they could not have doubted who he was. In this peculiar community created by the children at Turkowice, hierarchies and dependencies formed spontaneously, and there were some boys who subordinated others to themselves and sometimes exploited them. In the life of this community those who possessed leadership abilities played a special role; it was they who gathered their classmates around them and organized their activities. There were at least several warlords (found naturally among the group of older boys) whom everyone knew and sometimes even admired. The younger ones looked up to them, at times with fascination, at times with misgivings or even fear. Jasio the Redhead was not one of the warlords; for obvious reasons he could not have been. Neither was he, however, one of those who hid in the corners, whose constant fantasy was to find a magic cloak that would grant invisibility, or if not complete invisibility, at least an existence concealed by shadows. He was here, there, and everywhere, and the intense redness of his hair made it easy to notice and remember him. Soon enough he took on a certain role among his classmates: they respected him, and he occupied a relatively high position in the informal hierarchy so vital in a group of young or teenage boys. He did not lead, but rather joined; he forged bonds, and this, too, matters in a community of this kind.

When today, more than half a century later, my thoughts return to Jasio the Redhead, one thing above all intrigues me: his intense and spontaneous will to live, which in the season of great dying allowed him to evade death, to slip from death's thickly laid snares, to avoid the trap that closed after just one false move. I'm intrigued by the will to live that allowed him to bear the most intense suffering and precluded collapse or resignation for even a moment. Perhaps he realized that any loss or even diminution of energy augmented the chances of—and could equate to passive consent to—death. Until a certain moment, he was successful, and he must have hoped that, having reached Turkowice, he would prevail, endure, and live to see the war's end. Yet it happened otherwise. He was killed. He was killed just before the Germans abandoned the area—not by German hands, but by Ukrainian ones. He was killed not as a Jew, which might then have seemed peculiar or blatantly paradoxical; one could even treat such a death as a sign of the irony of fate, an irony violating the order established during the Holocaust. Jasio the Redhead was murdered along with Sister Longina and several other boys. That terrible event deserves its own telling.

※

The Death of Sister Longina

This murder has already been written about, and I won't repeat what can be read, all the more so as it seems to me that
not everything in these accounts corresponds to the actual course
of events, that in places their authors relied upon the deceptive
memory of those who were in Turkowice at the time. In principle
I do not intend to make any corrections. I have no qualifications
or authorization for doing so, and there are many things I simply
don't know, I don't command full knowledge of everything that
happened. At that time, in the spring of 1944, I was not yet ten
years old, I was fearful and stupefied, and in this sense my cog-
nitive horizon was circumscribed, flattened. I investigated nothing on my own but rather only absorbed what was said around
me and what it befell me to observe in my immediate surroundings, those directly in my sphere of vision. I can tell of these
events only in the form in which I perceived them at the time,
and so this will be a tale of how I saw that bleak history then and
how it embedded itself in my consciousness, rather than a re-
construction of the history itself.

Of everything that occurred in Turkowice during my stay
there, this was beyond a doubt the most horrible. I couldn't but
have been shocked by that crime, I couldn't have failed to remember it, even if only because its victims were people from my
immediate surroundings, people I saw constantly and knew
well. Although still young, we already knew that the world was

terrible and cruel—this was understood by all of us and belonged to each of our experiences, for the war had bypassed no
one, we could not remain anaesthetized and indifferent. Those
like myself who had experienced life in the ghetto had encountered iniquity directly, but even those who (for obvious reasons)
had not had this experience had nonetheless brushed against it.
For them as well this was evidence that crimes did not only occur far away, that they need not touch only others, that iniquity
was not an abstraction. The radiance of that menace embraced
each of us; there was no one who could feel safe in those times.

It was incontestably the most traumatic event in the wartime
annals of Turkowice. The convent sat in seclusion, on scorched
and abandoned land, cut off from the outside world and left to
its own devices. Yet like everything and everyone in the occupied country, it was vulnerable to repression and persecution, to
crime and violence. Nothing protected Turkowice from the incursions of Germans or the exploits of Ukrainian partisans, and
this kind of contact with the world could bring nothing apart
from suffering and misfortune. When the convent grew still
more impoverished, and critical items such as basic medicines
and soap were ever scarcer, it became necessary to set out in search
of assistance to the small neighboring town of Hrubieszów, distant by barely more than a dozen kilometers, but in those times
difficult to reach and thus far away. The mission was entrusted
to Sister Longina—why to her in particular, I don't know. Perhaps she volunteered, or perhaps she was regarded as the most
energetic and courageous; although the nuns who brought children from Warsaw, Sister Hermana among others, had on many
occasions provided impressive evidence of their courage, dedication, and self-sacrifice. Possibly the deciding factor was age: Sister Longina was relatively, if not very, young.

Nuns of various ages lived and worked in Turkowice. Sister
Stefania was the eldest; she was a figure associated with the January Uprising, perhaps because she was born in 1863 or because
her early childhood fell during that period. The elderly woman
was rarely seen, for she no longer worked. The nuns showed her

enormous respect, they treated her as if she were an ark joining the present with the distant past; she was a repository of the Turkowice convent and the entire holy order. More than half a century separated Sister Stefania from the youngest, Sisters Róża and Longina. Youth must have been among the factors playing a role in Mother Superior's decision to entrust Sister Longina with this difficult and precarious assignment.

When I came to Turkowice in early 1944, I was assigned to the third group, looked after by Sister Róża. Sister Longina worked with the second group, and while I had no direct contact with her, I saw her every day, as the groups' rooms were adjacent and their entrances were along the same corridor. I can't say very much about what Sister Longina looked like—she was thin, almost certainly blond, that's all. I can't say much not only because I have a poor visual memory, but also because the nuns' faces disappeared to some extent behind their large wimples, which were well starched and always, even during the worst times, spotlessly white, conspicuous for a wonderful cleanness that stood in contrast to all surrounding objects. The wimples of the Sister Maidservants of the Holiest Virgin Mary differed from those of the Sisters of Charity in that they did not point fancifully upward; instead they enveloped the head more closely and had a part at the bottom protruding outward in a way resembling a beak. The nuns wore their wimples all the time, in all situations, even when engaged in hard labor, despite the fact that the wimples must not have facilitated such tasks. Of course their facial features were visible, but they were confined, flattened.

Sister Longina was to set out for Hrubieszów with practical aims, to take care of concrete things, to obtain something for the convent, which was sinking into ever more precarious destitution. In accounts of this event the task apparently involved escorting to Hrubieszów the mother of a young nun who had died of tuberculosis. Here I am certain and can step forward to correct earlier reports: no nuns died in Turkowice during my stay there. Had something like this happened, I would definitely remember. The funeral, the days of mourning, the memories of the one who passed away would have fixed themselves in my consciousness. And I remember only one funeral—that of a young girl who died of consumption (her name, if I'm not mistaken, was Krysia Moćko); after the requiem mass, we formed a funeral procession and brought her to a nearby village cemetery. It seems to me that the nun with lung disease had died several years earlier, and that at that time, one of the nuns, perhaps even Sister Longina, had accompanied the mother after the funeral on her return trip home. If this had been the goal of the expedition ending in disaster, it would be necessary to ask what had happened to the mother. Was she also murdered (the accounts are silent about this), or was she allowed to go free—which would seem unlikely, for what kind of criminals would allow an eyewitness to remain alive? I think events from different times are being conflated here. What is certain is only that Sister Longina, together with the boys accompanying her, was murdered.

When the news spread of this expedition, there were many who wanted to take part in it; immediately there were volunteers. The nuns decided that the older boys could go, but only those who distinguished themselves, who were polite, even-tempered, responsible, in short, the best ones. I don't know how many of them there were in the end—some speak of seven, others of eight, and still others of nine. Nor do I remember their names (apart from Jasio the Redhead), perhaps because none of them came from Sister Róża's group. The boys must have been intended to provide protection—although as it was quickly revealed, they had no way to defend anyone against aggression—as well as indispensable assistance. By that time Turkowice had been severed from the world and there was no connection to Hrubieszów, as the narrow-gauge railway had not been operating for several months. There was only a smallish carriage called a trolley, it seems that at one time it had been equipped with an engine, which now was either broken or lacked fuel; in any case, the carriage had to be pushed by hand. And it must have been for this reason that so many boys accompanied Sister Longina.

She departed early in the morning, from the very beginning

accompanied by anxieties, for the trip was dangerous. Unless I am mistaken, prayers for the expedition's auspicious conclusion began right away in the chapel. We knew of the dangers, and all of our thoughts were with Sister Longina and our classmates. As the planned time of their return receded further into the past and they failed to come back, the increasing tension in the air became palpable, our anticipation grew more dramatic from hour to hour, our dread intensified. We prayed fervently, in earnest absorption, and raised humble entreaties. They went unheard. Our hopes dissolved, and the worst prophecies grew magnified: something terrible must have happened. Yet did we in Turkowice realize then that it had come to the worst?

It was only several days later that we learned of the murder. I don't remember how we learned of it or who brought the woeful news. In my memory there is only the impression the news evoked, an impression that was enormous and in essence difficult to describe, for me as well, even though I was already accustomed to learning of the death of people I had known only recently, and for me this situation was nothing new. I don't think the details and circumstances were yet known, only one thing was certain: the crime had been committed by Ukrainians, who wanted to cleanse the area of everyone they did not regard as their own. For them the young Polish nun and the underage boys accompanying her were enemies who had to be dealt with ruthlessly. Prayers of mourning commenced, but there could be no funeral because no one knew what the murderers had done with the bodies. As I later discovered, the bodies were recovered only after decades; they were found, if I'm not mistaken, in a roadside ditch. So the stories of the victims in those years are so often stories of the unburied.

I'm unable to say very much about Sister Longina's death. I looked upon what had occurred from the position of a child, by a child's very nature not grasping the course of events in its complexity, my observation was necessarily circumscribed, and only fragments of what took place reached me. Yet certain things were beyond doubt. In Turkowice I lived in a world of religious images, and the history more or less iconographically presented to us was a sacred history, one full of sacrifices and martyrdoms, and heroism in the battle for holy truth. In our minds Sister Longina was similar to the holy martyrs of the early Christian era, if not actually one of them. And the boys killed with her were reminiscent of those brave and pious young men whom the pagans had sentenced to death, dispatched by myrmidons to be devoured by lions.

There was still something else of tremendous importance: Sister Longina's martyrdom was an unceasing reminder of the dangers it had befallen us to live amidst and came to prefigure what fate could portend for all of us. Late spring and early summer of 1944 was the time of the greatest tension and danger for the Turkowice convent. This reached its culmination when news spread that Ukrainian nationalist divisions operating in the area intended to do away with it. The case of Sister Longina left no room for illusions, what this doing away with would consist of was clear in advance. Once again I don't know how news of these threats reached us, or how it came to be that Mother Superior reached a decision—undoubtedly in agreement with the Home Army division operating in the surrounding forests—to evacuate the convent. I can only tell of the events I took part in, which remain before my eyes in a form as vivid as if they occurred not more than half a century ago, but rather in the recent past.

Everything had been prepared, and it was decided that we would set off right after lunch, at two o'clock. It was a cool, dismal day, and both the children and the adults bustled about in anxiety and excitement. Roles and tasks had been assigned. What the convent owned was extremely worn-out, and in more normal times these things would have been on the verge of being discarded, but those dilapidated utensils, pieces of clothing, and other basic items continued to serve us, and we had to take along everything of any value or any use for existence in the woods.

As two o'clock drew near, we gathered in front of the building, preparing to form an evacuation march heading in the direction of that vast, kind forest controlled by the Polish underground army, when something entirely unexpected happened, a true *coup de théâtre*. From one moment to the next, literally at the last minute, Mother Superior changed her mind: we were staying! The news must have somehow reached her that the threats hanging over us had been staved off. I didn't know what had actually happened; to this day I don't know what caused the situation to be so radically transformed. At once the tension dissipated. Some of the boys were disappointed, as in their imaginations they had conjured up life in the woods as a great adventure. The tension dissipated because, after all, we had realized that in setting off into the unknown, we also had to be prepared for the worst. What had befallen Sister Longina and her companions could also happen to us. Mother Superior's sudden decision meant a certain return to normality, even though it was a normality on scorched earth amid hostile elements. During that quasi-normality, we could not forget about the deaths of Sister Longina and the boys. Soon, though, the rapid speed of events and the multiplication of threats caused the fate of the expedition to Hrubieszów to lose its piercing topicality and slip into the past.

✻

On a Sunday Morning

That day it seemed to me that the world was—if only slightly—less terrible and threatening than usual. We had beautiful summer weather, warm and mild, not sweltering, the sun, unobscured by even a single cloud, let me gaze more clearly at my own condition, at what was around me. I left the house and walked outside. The space just behind the house had been long neglected, yet neglect had not entirely effaced all traces of its former splendor, the space still bore signs of having once been transformed from a chaotic scrawlation of weeds, shrubs, and other self-sufficient forms of vegetation unconcerned about human care into a garden. Amid this chaos of untended plants there surely remained some that had once been properly cared for, since the contours of some rows, the outlines of some flower beds, were still visible. Convent legend spoke of how, in those not-so-long-ago but already distant times described by the (concise, yet laden with meaning and even magical) expression "before the war," there had been a marvelous garden here, overflowing with flowers beautiful and fragrant, seducing—as in fairy tales—visitors with their wondrous colors, praising God by their very existence. Even now there was some vegetation in bloom, but this was no longer a carefully arranged and pampered cloister garden; the nuns, confronted with so many new and difficult tasks, were overworked and exhausted, and were constantly scrambling to ensure that the convent harboring some three hundred children would survive this terrible time at all. So they had neither the energy nor the ability to concern themselves with this, too. Roses are not tended to when the world is falling apart, when dangers are drawing near from various sides, when procuring even the most basic things is impossible without an intensified effort, an effort so great that years later it is difficult even to imagine.

The nuns must have planted some flowers, because there were many of them—especially at this time of year—adorning the chapel, and these were surely not only the wildflowers abundant in the world outside. In the winter this adornment was naturally much more modest, although on holidays dried flowers would still appear. Today, though, when my memory tries to encompass that space behind our house, the house where we boys lived, I can concede that while it might have embodied the shape of a garden, it was already bare but fertile—wild greenery must have prospered there.

The chapel on the second floor of our house was the place of greatest importance, forming the center of a world then almost hermetically sealed. The tiny wooden church standing nearby, toward the river, had undergone dramatic vicissitudes and been closed; when it later reopened its doors to the faithful, the reconsecration ceremony was splendiferous, the occasion of the first church fair held in Turkowice in years. Naturally the chapel was the most important place for the nuns, but it was also the most important place for the convent's wards, for myself as well. I went there often. I found there something that set this place apart from all others open to me at the time; it was clear, calm, and orderly and possessed a sense all other places were lacking. On that Sunday morning, I found myself in this space whose general appearance I am trying to convey, just after leaving the chapel, after (as was usually the case on Sundays) a long, solemn ceremonial and mass. The harmonium resounded only during such services; one of the older girls, perhaps already twenty years old, performed the hymns in a pleasant soprano. I didn't then know that the world of sounds would so come to fascinate me, yet music already brought me much pleasure, and the sensations it evoked were powerful ones, so different from the sensations otherwise assailing me from all around. The chapel was the one place where the sublime was made manifest.

And on that Sunday in July, in this gently elevated mood, I walked outside to the smallish space extending out behind our house. In attempting here to recall it, I'm aware that even while its image has here and there been effaced, my memory has mastered it quite well, and there remain very few bare or undefined fragments inclining more to the proliferation of question marks than to confident description. And hence opposite our building stood the house where the girls lived, smaller, yet nonetheless—given conditions in Turkowice—impressive. The path joining these houses, which once surely must have been the main path through the garden, formed the axis of that space, separating it into two distinct parts. On one side of the girls' house stood a small building called—as far as I remember—the washhouse; on the other side, but farther back, so that most likely it couldn't be seen from where I lived, stood a small cottage. A mysterious man lived there. We didn't know who he was, perhaps he was in hiding. Behind the girls' house began the pine forest, not overly dense, but composed of tall, willowy pines shooting into the sky. This was the kingdom of the crows, which nested here in enormous flocks. The boys, driven by hunger, would climb those tapering pine trees and steal eggs and fledgling crows from the nests.

On the left side, amid lush shrubs, stood the "isolation ward." This was the small convent infirmary, which was no longer functioning, given the absence of both doctors and basic medicines. Behind it, beyond the convent's enclosure, the land sloped gently toward the Huczwa River, although the road to the river did not pass this way. And beyond the river were the woods, which were thick and vast, and seemed to me limitless and mysterious, dark and impenetrable. I knew, as we all did, that these woods were full of activity, that the partisans operated there and from there set out to battle. This naturally excited the imagination, and inclined some of the boys, especially the older ones, to dream of escaping the prosaic life of the convent and joining those who fought heroic battles.

Most difficult for me to describe is that edge of the rectangle situated vis-à-vis the isolation ward; I remember very little of it, I'm unable to say what had once been there, for what remained was bare and ill defined. Or was there, perhaps, nothing distinctive on that side, nothing that would clearly define that space? The village extended farther, a village it was then possible to speak of only in the past tense, because it had been emptied of its population and there remained only remnants of buildings and traces of a once-exuberant life. The scorched-earth policy had been applied here, and those Polish peasants who had escaped with their lives had moved to outlying areas. I remember a quite distant cemetery, some rotting granaries. . . . And there perhaps was talk of a Jewish orchard. It belonged to a Jew who had been murdered several years earlier, and now the orchard was deserted and neglected, cultivated by no one. It was a bit farther away, and I'd never been there. When I think now about that rectangular area between the two main houses, forming the center of the convent's land, and about myself on that beautiful Sunday morning, I realize that I'm unable to make out the quarters of the globe, I don't know which direction was south and which was north, where west lay as opposed to east. I don't know and am unable now to reconstruct this, even though at that time when I was there, I must not have had any doubts, especially on a day as bright as that Sunday, when it seemed to me that the terrible, cruel world was a bit less infernal.

I was alone after mass, as my companions had dispersed; perhaps they took off for the river, or the woods, or other sites of frequent visitation. I avoided venturing any distance from the convent—it seemed to me that proximity was the best refuge—however, that morning I was about to learn that for me there were no nonthreatening places. And so I was circling that space which had once been a garden and feeling relatively well. Not only was the beautiful weather on my side, I thought, but also the unexpected solitude. I was away from that ceaselessly clamoring herd to which fate had joined me. I never forgot that I was something in the way of a hunted animal, which anyone—if it so pleased him—could shoot, trample, or annihilate in any other way, including the most imaginative. But I was not thinking of that just then. I was calmer than at any other time, and it didn't enter my mind that in a moment something would happen that would reduce my calm, then so rarely attained, to ashes.

At a certain moment the three brothers Z. appeared in my field of vision. This didn't surprise me; evidently they, too, had stayed near the convent after mass. I knew them, because we all knew each other; they were in another group, though, so I had not had close contact with them. I knew that they were originally from Warsaw and that they had been brought to Turkowice shortly before I had, just a few months earlier (my group, which came with Sister Hermana from Warsaw, was the last). The brothers were almost always seen together; the youngest was my age, and the eldest, I would guess, five years older. This fifteen-year-old was clearly the leader of the family, while the two younger brothers submitted unquestioningly to him, playing the roles he assigned them. I don't remember their names, yet it seems to me that the leader was named Jurek.

I didn't have long to wait. They surrounded me as if they wanted to form a snare and render impossible my escape. It came as a surprise, I didn't know what was going on or what they could want from me, I'd never gotten in their way. I would learn quickly what it was they had to say to me, for they did not delay. The eldest spoke up (a hierarchy obtained among them, and only he could impart such a message): "We know you're a Jew. The Germans will be here tomorrow. We'll tell them, and they'll put you in your place."

Of course after so many years have passed I'm not certain that these were the precise words, yet the meaning I am conveying faithfully, it imprinted itself deeply upon my memory. I remember the terror the oldest brother Z.'s outburst evoked in me. I had no illusions. They had decided to send me to my death, for I knew well that this kind of pronouncement was not a groundless threat. I was petrified, my good mood dissolved at once, I no longer thought of the beautiful weather or of the sun and the greenery—my world once again grew black, it returned to normal. Fear paralyzed me. I stood motionless, as if rooted to the ground—and not only because the brothers Z. surrounded me. Fear rendered me powerless. Earlier experiences had already taught me that fear renders one powerless especially when it's understood that life is at stake—and in those times there were no lower stakes, they simply didn't enter into consideration. When today I tell of this event from years ago, it seems to me there's no way to describe this most basic fear, a fear so thoroughly piercing that it belongs to those experiences evading language, laying bare the flatness, the inadequacy, and the incommensurability of words. For years I hoped to find a description of such fear in the great works of literature, yet I never came upon it, and I suspect it simply does not exist. For me to attempt such a description would be an act of conceit and presumptuousness, and likewise naïveté, given that the undertaking would be predestined to failure. Fear, and in particular the kind I speak of here, arising from the most basic threats, defies description. I can only say that I grew alternately hot and cold, my knees buckled, a strange current passed through my legs, and my heart beat more quickly than usual. Physicians perhaps will research the physiology of fear and present an account of their discoveries relying upon specialists' terminology; when confronted with such tasks, everyday words stand as powerless as, in most cases, does the person who finds himself in mortal danger.

I will say, tritely, that after what I heard from the brothers Z., fear seized me with its claws. I was silent, I didn't respond in any way to that dictum. Persuading them that this was nonsense, that I wasn't a Jew, would have been futile, it could only have irritated and provoked them. Nor would it have made sense to plead with them not to do that, that it would end badly for me and after all, I had done nothing to them. It would have made no sense because it would have constituted an admission, and this was not to be done under any pretext. Such held true in this case as well, for an admission could only confirm the brothers Z. in their zealous intent, which they had presented to me point-blank and with such clarity. I was young, a child, yet accidents of fate had already instilled in me the wisdom of remaining silent when speaking was not an absolute necessity. Speaking, particularly about oneself, could only be harmful. This principle I had internalized deeply; as in this case, I managed to adhere to it even in grave situations.

When years afterward I reflect on this event, which so suddenly and radically destroyed the good mood that had unexpectedly been mine and transformed that beautiful Sunday morning into a nightmare, naturally I think about my own reactions. Yet I'm curious as well about my three persecutors, about the reasons and motivations for their behavior. What prompted them to do this? It was doubtlessly *un acte gratuit*. There was no question of blackmail, because they wanted and expected nothing from me—nor could they have, for I had at my disposal nothing of any value, and precisely this disinterestedness renders it impossible to call them *szmalcownicy*. Of course they realized that if they were to do this, they would be condemning me to death. This much was clear during the occupation years—it belonged to elementary knowledge, accessible even to browbeaten urchins. Yet I don't know whether they understood that they would also be injuring many others, above all the nuns, but also their other classmates, and not necessarily only those who were Jewish and in hiding. Perhaps they didn't think of this? Or perhaps it was just this that they wished to do, to take revenge on their surroundings, which for some reason they detested? I don't know and am definitely never to learn, I won't delve into their motives, and I'm unable to recreate them. I'm convinced of one thing: this was not an ordinary act of intimidation, and thus was not an immature prank, free of consequences. During the occupation such pronouncements carried a weight of their own, and they could not be even the most foolish and cruel joke; such knowledge was universally accessible, and the three brothers must have possessed it. With complete certainty the eldest did.

I think coming into play here was pure, perhaps wholly un-reflective, hatred, bound up with the spirit of the time or ema-nating from it. Not by chance do I invoke this here. When all is said and done, the *Zeitgeist* sanctioned the conviction that some-one exposed as a Jew was a priori condemned to death, destined for the firing squad. Not only was Jewish life cheap, it was of no consequence. It had become dispossessed of any value. Moreover, anyone, even if he didn't himself belong to the master race, could conclude that causing someone to lose his Jewish life was not a sin and was nothing at all to be reproached for—perhaps it even constituted a praiseworthy act. It seems to me that at least the oldest brother Z., who was raised on the streets of Warsaw, com-prehended the spirit of the time perfectly and had assimilated it, regarding its lessons, including the practical ones, as natural and self-evident. Somehow he had reached the conclusion—on the basis of observation, some kind of reasoning or another, or conjecture—that I was a Jew, and no longer did he harbor any doubts as to what ought to be done. The cruelty of an epoch is concentrated and reflected in the cruelties of children, who mirror the villainy committed in the adult world, this case was a simple reenactment. And teachings emanating from other sources were not always able to counteract this spirit of the time. On that Sunday morning the brothers Z. had been in the chapel attending the same service that I had, doubtlessly they heard about loving thy neighbor during the sermon. Perhaps they turned a deaf ear to those words and declined to take them into consideration, yet I would suppose that it happened otherwise. In their consciousness the world was divided into rigidly sepa-rated partitions bearing no relationship to one another, and therefore what might be important and even obligatory in one partition failed to apply in another. The lessons imparted by the priest and nuns, and the spirit of the time, belonged to disparate, noncontiguous realities.

Of course these are my reflections today. At the time, on that sunny morning, I didn't ask myself what had led the brothers Z. to treat me as they did. It was sufficient for me to know that they were among those wanting to send me to my death, among those from whom I had to flee, from whom I had to defend myself if I wanted to live, for I was perfectly aware of what denunciation to the Germans meant for me. And after all, there were more important questions. I had to decide what to do, how to behave in the face of a threat that meant the end—and could mean nothing else. I had very little time. Of what the oldest brother Z. told me, I was most struck by the news that the Germans were to arrive the next day. This had to be taken seriously, even though one had to wonder how the brothers Z. had come to know of it. In recent months the Germans had no longer appeared in secluded Turkowice, yet their previous savage exploits remained in vivid memory. And that they had not appeared by no means meant that they would not appear. After all, wasn't it still the case that they could do what they wanted to?

Therefore I had to make up my mind, I had to reach a decision. Should I submit passively to fate, say nothing to anyone about what the brothers Z. had announced to me, wait for what was to come—and in a flush of optimism believe that now, as before, I would be spared? At first I thought this was what I would do, because I saw no other possibility. What choice did I have? Yet within a short time I began to consider another solution. I would flee from Turkowice, where the Germans were to arrive the next day and kill me, I would run to the largest and densest forest on the other side of the river, and in the woods—one could hope—the Germans would not catch me. To be sure, there were others there who would also like to do away with me, but perhaps I would come across a friendly and protective division, one of the Polish partisan units who had assisted our convent and taken it under their care; at times some of these soldiers would come and confer for a long time with Mother Superior. After a while, though, I was seized by fear when I realized that I would find myself alone in a vast and dark and, above all, strange forest, where even if I did not die from a German or a Ukrainian bullet, I would lose my way and die just the same. I would have nothing to eat and I would constantly be exposed to adversities

I wasn't even able to imagine, for until then I had never encountered untamed nature, I came from the city and lacked even
the most basic sense of bearings in the enormous forest.

As I reconstruct those moments today, as I extract them from
the depths of my memory, weighed down by other events and experiences, I'm able to discern that despite the tension and terror,
I did try to consider various possibilities and seek out the most
favorable solution, although none was good. Fear does not always
exclude rational thinking. I don't know how long I mused over
that escape into the woods, perhaps it was only a moment, perhaps it was fifteen minutes or an hour. In any case I abandoned
that idea, growing certain that it was not for me. I wasn't yet ten,
yet I stood before a kind of decision that in somewhat more normal times even adults would rarely face—it was in fact a matter
of life and death. I had already known extreme situations, I had
very nearly been packed into a freight car on Umschlagplatz carrying its passengers on a final journey to Treblinka, but at that
time the decision was made by adults, I merely yielded to them.
And now, having been shocked in the convent's courtyard by so
terrifying an announcement, an unambiguous death sentence, I
was left on my own.

It seemed to me there was no one I could turn to for aid and
counsel. Then after a while I thought that, after all, there was
someone: the only people I knew of who wanted what was good
for me, whom I could trust, were the nuns and the priest, I would
find out from them what I should do, and I would follow their instructions. Although I knew my question was important, I would
not have dared to turn to Mother Superior. She enjoyed the highest authority and was someone whose every word counted and
carried enormous weight, I and everyone else in Turkowice knew
that it fell to her to make the gravest decisions; she was not,
though, in daily contact with the children, rather she was absorbed in matters of general planning and ceaseless, exhausting
efforts to maintain the convent. Neither would I have dared to
tell the priest what had happened to me. From my perspective
then he existed on summits wholly inaccessible to me. Of the

brothers' threats I resolved to tell Sister Róża. She was the preceptress of the group to which I was assigned, and I knew her the best.

I began to search for her feverishly, so as to tell her as quickly as I could of the threat hanging over me, but I couldn't find her. That beautiful Sunday morning was definitely not a rest period for Sister Róża. At certain times of the day the nuns would gather in the chapel for prayers prescribed by the rules of the convent, and at such times the chapel was inaccessible to us; at other times, it seemed to me, they devoted themselves to meditation in the refectory, where entrance was in general prohibited. But perhaps she was in that small, partitioned area where the beehives were kept? For not only was Sister Róża the preceptress of our group, she was also engaged with bee-keeping, which constituted the only tolerably functioning remnant of the prewar farm; I didn't think, though, that she devoted herself to such labors on Sundays. I searched for her more and more nervously, with ever greater impatience, even though I knew that I would find her before long, since the nuns who worked directly with the children never withdrew for any length of time.

Finally she approached. I went to her right away, and from my flustered state she must have guessed at once that I had come to her with something grave and momentous. I didn't want to speak in the hallway, having by then learned the principles of conspiracy, I knew that no one not called upon—that is, my classmates—should hear of this, for then it would be still worse. Sister Róża went with me to a place called the storage room, another part of her domain (at that time the name was in essence a matter of custom, since the household objects that would be stored there were lacking). I set forth in detail the brothers Z.'s threat, and asked her what I should do. I heard that I was not to worry, since no one had said anything about the Germans' coming to Turkowice the next day, the nuns were not expecting any further incursions. And even if they were to come to Turkowice, the brothers Z. would certainly not do what they had proclaimed. They would be summoned and would hear that such things were impermissible. And I think that very soon, still that Sunday, they were summoned—and before the countenance of Mother Superior herself. Of course I don't know what they heard there, yet I do suppose that forceful words were uttered. I'm unable to say how long I spent in the storage room. I suspect it was a short time. In the end something unanticipated occurred that was of utter significance, among other reasons, because it convinced me in a tangible way that the brothers Z., who wanted to send me to certain death, were not the only ones in the world. Sister Róża took from the cupboard a slice of bread, smeared it with butter (I noticed that the remainder was kept in a small clay pot), and handed it to me, saying that I should eat it here, at once. There was no need for more prodding; at that time there was ever greater hunger in the convent, bread was rigidly apportioned and had become the object of incessant desire, and butter had become something entirely unfamiliar, perhaps its very existence had been forgotten. That chunk of wholemeal bread (there was no other kind in Turkowice) was something more than a piece of food serving to satisfy hunger— it transformed itself into a sign imparting to me that there were people here who were kind to me, that the world was not so monstrous as it had seemed a few minutes earlier. And Sister Róża's gesture has lasted in my memory perhaps still more powerfully than her reassuring words, to this day I think of it with gratitude. Thanks to it I felt safer, although of course I could not be certain that the brothers Z. would not fulfill their cruel declaration.

I don't remember what I did during the remaining hours of that beautiful July Sunday, most likely nothing that would fall outside of daily routine. I think I sat, doing nothing, in the room assigned to our group, and as usual holed myself up in a corner, dreaming of being unnoticed, invisible. I did not flee to any of the surrounding forests. I did not even step into that area of the convent's property between the girls' house and main house (where the chapel, Mother Superior's office, and a kitchen in the cellar were located, and where the boys lived). After all that had happened to me that day, I would have been unable to contemplate that space, the lush greenery would not have moved me, the sun's rays, effecting a particular transparency in the summer air, would have brought me no joy. During moments of great danger and internal fracture, a person fails to perceive the external world—even that which is nearest and most beautiful ceases to exist—it transforms itself into a void. Even if the outside world does not vanish, this is still more upsetting, since it remains disjoined from what is most important and what truly matters. On that Sunday I ceased to perceive the world around me. I still bore the weight of what the brothers Z. had told me, and while I had grown somewhat calmer after the conversation with Sister Róża, I continued to feel more vulnerable than usual, and naturally could not be entirely convinced that they would not do what they had threatened if the Germans were actually to invade our convent the next day.

Yet fortunately nothing of this kind occurred. The Germans did not come on Monday, and they did not come on the following days. They never again appeared in Turkowice. Something began to change, and after some time, not long, we could hear the first echoes of the front, detonations and repeated gunshots resounding in the distance. The battles drew nearer, we didn't know if they would pour over into our area. The boys were waiting for just this, they wanted to see what a real war looked like and perhaps even to join in it. The nuns had been preparing for impending events, and when the front drew near, they ordered us to stay in the extensive cellars, worried that the front would pass through Turkowice. They worried about something else as well: they knew how the Bolsheviks had treated the clergy during the revolution, and they could not exclude the possibility that on Polish land, driven by atheist fanaticism and clouded by impiety, they would commit terrible deeds. At that time the nuns could no longer harbor any illusions. There would be no liberator arriving on a white horse.

The Red Army entered Turkowice without a battle, a division pitched its tents on nearby fields that were lying fallow. For several days the soldiers moved about our area, they were dirty and severely exhausted, and they rolled cigarettes from shag tobacco and scraps of old newspapers. They behaved decently, and at moments even amicably. They showed their rifles to the boys, who were enormously intrigued by all of this—and after some time they disappeared. I cannot say a bad word about them. They did not confirm the nuns' dark anticipations. Nothing at all happened that could be linked to any kind of threat to the convent.

How did I react to these events? I think that I was still so intimidated and stupefied that I failed to appreciate their significance, either in general or for myself. And I definitely did not formulate the triumphant or contented thought: "I survived the war." Perhaps this was because the war here had in essence not yet ended, it had only become somewhat different, assumed other forms; someone called it small, yet small need not mean nonthreatening. On the surface there were no fundamental changes in my immediate situation, and yet everything had changed—and radically. At the time I was certainly, even if only subconsciously, aware of this, today I perceive it explicitly. The entry of the armies from the east is no longer spoken of as "liberation," some say "the so-called liberation," and others use still more forceful expressions, calling everything that happened a second occupation. I must say with complete openness and sincerity: for me, regardless of whether I was or was not fully aware of this in the summer of 1944, the entry of the Russians was liberation. And I am still prepared to think this way today, even though I'm aware of the entanglements and tremendous variety of abominable things that were to follow. Someone in my situation could not perceive things otherwise—the threat of immediate death for reasons of race, blood, or something similar ceased. I could be certain that the brothers Z. would never again threaten me with the taunt "We'll turn you over to the Germans." One might claim that this is insufficient justification for such a perception of history. Yet for me it was much, very much. It meant life.

✿

A Louse on a Beret, a Chasuble, a Pair of Shoes

It was a cold and dismal day in February, in no way distinctive, I could not have dreamt that this particular day would become so important, would weigh so radically on my life. I wasn't expecting or counting on anything; in general I didn't think about the possibility of any kind of change. My time in Turkowice was homogeneous and arrested, shaped on a certain model that seemed inviolable, if not eternal. I was aware, of course, that there were no longer Germans here, but I didn't think about whether the war was coming to an end, I lived from one gray day to the next—and this banal winter morning failed to depart in any way from the others. As usual I sat on the bench, busy doing nothing and thinking about nothing, indifferent and stupefied. At a certain moment one of the boys came into the room and called out to me: "Your mother's come."

I didn't react to those words, I didn't take them seriously, they failed to extricate me from my indifference, give me pause, or wrest me from the bench where I sat. I supposed that the boy was taunting me and deceiving me for reasons best known to himself, perhaps just to upset me. I was distrustful of everyone and everything, including claims of occurrences that could disturb the daily routine, which was so completely stabilized, in fact ossified. I knew that the arrival of a family member, especially a mother, was one of the incessant dreams the boys lived by, a fantasy irresistible to even the toughest ones, to whom, it might seem, all sentimental daydreams were alien. Nothing, however, of this sort had happened in a long time. The last case had occurred a long time ago, in the summer of the previous year, before the Russians arrived. The mother of one boy had come and taken him to Warsaw. This was much talked about, so much so that to this day I remember the name of that fortunate one who was able to leave the Turkowice convent and return to his family: his name was Wiercioch. Shortly afterward, though, the news reached us that an uprising had broken out in Warsaw, that on the streets battles were being fought and people were dying, and then he ceased to be thought of as an object of jealousy and the chosen one of fate. We didn't know what had happened to him; perhaps he had been killed, since terrible things were happening there, whereas of late Turkowice had been quite safe and calm. There was consolation in this, as if it confirmed that, after all, life in the convent was not the most terrible—but unless I am mistaken, no one ceased to fantasize about breaking away.

As for myself, I'd grown deadened and indifferent and had most likely lost even the ability to fantasize. Moreover I knew that the world I'd known before my arrival, the world in which I'd once lived, no longer existed, and that behind me was empty space and nothingness. I didn't think about this world, and I didn't return to the past, in an odd way I'd expelled it from my consciousness, and my existence was limited to what was here and now. Nor did I think about whether anyone in my family was alive or whether I would ever see any of them again. For this reason, too, I didn't react to the sensational news one of my classmates tossed me from the doorway.

I took it seriously several minutes later, when Sister Róża told me the same thing. My mother was waiting for me on the second floor, in a small room that had once served as a guestroom. A short while later I was alone with her. I should have been mad for joy—an indescribable good fortune had come to me—and yet I was not capable of rejoicing, happiness transcended the repertoire of my behavior. I was so taken by surprise, so unable to absorb what was happening, that I was incapable of wresting from myself anything that would express it. So unexpected an event undoubtedly went beyond me. I was silent. I maintained a distance and restraint as if I had not just regained the person closest to me after a long separation. A year and some months earlier, parting with my mother had come as a shock to me. Now our first meeting after the war, a war from which she and I had miraculously escaped with our lives, also came as a shock, in its own way paralyzing. I made no gestures appropriate to such an extraordinary situation. I didn't throw my arms around her. I didn't know how to extract from myself so much as a single sentence that would have been spontaneous and, at the same time, appropriate in such circumstances. Only after a while did I say, "Mama, a huge louse is marching around on your beret." And in fact this was the first thing I noticed.

I know that in writing of this after so many decades, I am departing from conventions and violating the principle of commensurability. A mother's first encounter with her son after the most terrible of catastrophes ought to be sublime. Yet it was not so. My mother must have been disconcerted when she heard my words, for this was not what she had expected from me. At once she took off her old, terribly shabby beret and did away with the insect. Paradoxically, that louse enabled normal human contact; it enabled me to overcome my overawed state, and to some extent brought an extraordinary situation into the realm of the ordinary and quotidian. For insects were not foreign to me—I remembered them from the ghetto, and there was no dearth of them in Turkowice; the kitchen was subjugated by cockroaches, bedbugs and fleas were everywhere rampant, and abundant lice enjoyed comfortable lives. These hideous creatures unfailingly rise to the surface in all places where wars and misfortunes befall people, as if they were waiting for bad times, concealing themselves during better periods in nooks and corners, convinced that their era has not yet arrived. Black seasons are their times of prosperity.

My mother's miserable journey to Turkowice had lasted about two weeks. I don't know how it began, whether she set out from Otwock, where she was still living as a servant in the house beneath the eagles, or whether in searching for her surviving family she had first gone to Pruszków (a rendezvous point for those family members who had managed to survive the occupation). I didn't inquire about the details at the time, and later she was exceedingly restrained in her accounts; she disliked returning to those times and was not wont to speak about her own life, preferring to conceal herself in shadows. I am certain of one thing: immediately after the Germans' departure, my mother somehow made contact with her family. A prewar acquaintance from Pruszków, whose name was Kenigsztajn, planned to make his way to the eastern regions, and my mother was to go part of the way with him. He was setting out for Sokołów Podlaski, where he, together with his wife and two children, had survived by hiding for years in a dugout. Afterward, if I'm not mistaken, he was headed for some reason toward the area near Hrubieszów. My mother stayed in Sokołów for several days in order to set off together with him, but at the last moment he changed his plans, and she decided then that she would make her way to Turkowice alone. I'm unfamiliar with the details, yet I do know that the journey was ghastly, drawing out endlessly and exposing her to various atrocities and an accumulation of seemingly insurmountable difficulties. My mother traversed numerous stretches of road on foot; part of the way she traveled on a freight train transporting soldiers from the front who, pitying her, took her in. That she had no money at all complicated the situation further; Kenigsztajn, whose family was also impoverished, loaned her some small sum. That journey, requiring energy and rapid decision-making, was especially difficult for my mother, who was not resourceful and, above all, was timid. In such situations she lacked aggressiveness, she didn't know how to make contact with the potentially helpful chance acquaintance. Yet she was determined, and she knew that she would have to expose herself to setbacks and difficulties in order to reach that distant, out-of-the-way place. She'd had no news from me for a long time, yet she believed that I was alive and that she would be able to collect me from the nuns.

I think that when, exhausted and frozen, she at last reached her goal and learned that I was there, alive, that I had survived the war, she was happy. Happy, although as usual restrained, surely she didn't externalize her great joy. Nor am I convinced that I comprehended my good fortune. I was sufficiently lucid to notice a louse gliding along a beret, yet my senses were also dulled, and my imagination, as if frozen, had ceased to function, I didn't even reflect on whether I might spend the coming years outside of the Turkowice convent. Yet it turned out that I could not accompany my mother when she left the following day; the frost was biting and the difficulties of the journey were enormous, in essence, unforeseeable. Moreover I was ill. For some time I had been afflicted with pus-exuding boils burrowing deeply into my body, they had arisen from malnutrition. Even so I was fortunate, many of my classmates had been afflicted with something still worse: night blindness. When dusk fell, they grew unable to see.

I don't remember how I parted with my mother or how she got out of Turkowice, which at that time was an enclosed space separated from the rest of the world, yet I did know then that I was definitely not saying goodbye to her forever. Neither do I remember if I asked about my father. I hadn't seen him in over two years, but could I have forgotten about his existence? For a long time my mother had received no sign of life from him, she knew only that during a roundup in Kielce he had been seized on the street and transported to Germany. That he had survived we learned later, when the war was over and letters could travel back and forth. Before long, near the end of 1945, he returned to Poland to join us.

During her stay in Turkowice, which lasted no longer than a day, my mother spoke with Mother Superior, Father Bajka, and Sister Róża. She thanked them for having saved my life, for she judged reasonably that had the nuns not taken me in, likely I would not have lived through the time of the Holocaust. She thanked them, although she must have been aware that no words were capable of carrying the weight of the gratitude she wanted to instill in them. Language contains nothing that could be adequate in such situations. When the nuns asked if I had been baptized, she answered that I had not been—and immediately gave her consent to the baptism. There was no pressure on the part of either the nuns or the priest. Rather my mother—who, like many Jews who were assimilated or in the process of assimilating, was indifferent toward religion—believed that her consent would be the most meaningful act of thanks and gratitude. They agreed that she would come to Turkowice in three months, when the weather would be milder and the travel conditions perhaps more humane, while for my part I would recover from the boils. The ceremony of my inclusion in the body of disciples of the Catholic faith was to take place before her arrival.

No special lessons preceded the baptism. The nuns felt that I was well initiated in the sacred mysteries and that in practice I was already a Catholic, even before this symbolic act of fundamental significance was to be performed. Here I must tell of something of unusual importance: Mother Superior decided that Jewish children staying in Turkowice would be allowed to take part in all religious practices, and so would be treated just like all the other children who had belonged to the Catholic Church since birth. The rules of conspiracy demanded this, out of consideration for safety Jewish children could not stand out in any way. Still, I can imagine how difficult this decision was for the nuns. Many years later one of the girls who was at Turkowice with me spoke about this with Father Bajka, and he confessed to her that at the time he had been inclined to resist such a resolution, yet he knew now that it was the Holy Spirit who had guided Mother Superior when she understood that the problem had to be resolved in this way. These words bear a particular weight, especially having been uttered by a man of the cloth.

The ceremony lasted a short time. It took place in the spring, on a sunny afternoon, in Father Bajka's chamber, not merely without publicity, but in secret. Sister Róża called me into the so-called storage room so that I could change from my ragged everyday things into an outfit somewhat more appropriate to such an unusual and elevated moment, an outfit, it's true, that was also by then threadbare, reminiscent of older times, perhaps the twenties. Following the ceremony I was to come back to the storage room unseen and return the ceremonial attire. No one was to take notice of my baptism, it was necessary to avoid sensation and comment. At that time, in the spring of 1945, there were no longer Germans, and exposure of the fact that I was a Jew who had only here, in Turkowice, received baptism and become a Catholic, no longer brought the threat of death; even so, my classmates, had they learned of it, would have pointed fingers and embittered my life there.

After so many years I'm unable to reconstruct the feelings that this ceremony evoked in me. When I was brought to Turkowice at the beginning of 1944, I already had two brief stays in religious boarding schools behind me and was somewhat acquainted with Catholicism, yet this was only a superficial acquaintance, the world of Catholicism I entered only after my arrival. And it was the only period in my life when I was a believer, deeply devout, ensorcelled by religious images. Shortly after my departure from Turkowice, this sphere of experience closed itself to me, and faith disappeared as quickly as it had come. Years later I reflect on whether my sudden piety, while undoubtedly sincere, was not lined with a certain opportunism: in a spontaneous and unreflective way, I adapted to the norms obtaining in Turkowice and became a part of that world. The principle of mimesis also functioned here somewhat: in becoming so deeply devout, I not only won the favor and goodwill of the nuns, but also overcame my own alienness, even while I was not so fortunate to free myself from this entirely.

I suspect other considerations came into play as well. During the occupation faith could not bring someone such as myself a complete feeling of safety—this would have been a psychological luxury difficult not only to attain, but even to imagine—yet it did at least suggest that there existed some kind of order to the world, that goodness and meaning had not been cast out as refuse. The image of a protective and just God made it possible to better bear the daily negations of goodness and justice, to take consolation from the fact that this sinister and abominable world was not the only one. And above all, everything connected to religion was beautiful. The chapel remained the one bright, unsoiled, ordered place; it stood in contrast to the rest of Turkowice, it was a space apart from all others, belonging to another universe. It was in this chapel that I took part in rituals and ceremonies that captivated me with their uncommon and poetic qualities; it was here that I heard hymns, songs that seemed to me indescribably beautiful. I drank them in as if they were angelic descants. And I dreamt that I, too, would be an acolyte like some of my classmates and in this way would have higher, more direct contact with God. It was never my fortune, though, to have this kind of experience, even after my baptism.

In connection with this I must tell a certain story. The next day I went to the chapel for morning mass, and immediately I noticed that the priest was conducting the mass in a different chasuble than usual, one I had never seen before. It disconcerted me, caused me to wonder, raised questions I was unable to answer. I could not free myself from the thought that the chasuble was the same one it had previously been, only now, after the sacrament of baptism, I perceived it differently because I was now a new, different person. I didn't know what to make of this, I was faced with a question I couldn't resolve: did this always happen, was it a natural consequence of my official and complete accession to the Church, and thus its own kind of rule, or was it only myself whom God had distinguished in this way, allowing me—the transformed one—to see a metamorphosed world? The question tormented me all the more, because if the second were true, then I could consider myself to have encountered a miracle. And miracles were spoken of constantly, even if only in stories from the lives of saints, or for instruction and confirmation in faith.

The God we were taught about in Turkowice was not a concealed God. He was constantly engaging in events, he weighed on the world's fate and intervened in our daily lives. In the room belonging to the third group, a painting depicted Christ with an open heart, to which he pointed with his right hand. When we especially misbehaved or when something occurred that was particularly worthy of condemnation (it once happened that two of the boys were not at Sunday mass because they had run off to the woods to pick berries), Sister Róża would suggest that we look again, carefully, at Jesus's hand: was it not swelling? She didn't claim this authoritatively, but only pointed to the possibility, leaving the boys to discuss feverishly the question: was the hand swollen or not? The replies were varied, I didn't have an opinion of my own in this matter. Doubtlessly, though, I reasoned thus: insofar as Sister Róża spoke to us about such an eventuality, this meant that Jesus reacted directly to our actions, evaluated them, and when necessary expressed his dissatisfaction. Given this, then perhaps after my transformation, Jesus, satisfied, caused me to see the world differently.

I didn't know how to cope with this problem, or how to resolve it, it became my secret that I wished not to share with anyone. In truth I don't know why. Perhaps I was embarrassed, perhaps I was afraid (for I would have had to tell of the baptism that had taken place so recently in Father Bajka's chamber), or perhaps I simply feared being ridiculed. I relaxed only when I heard my classmates commenting on the fact that the priest was conducting holy mass in a new chasuble. I must have been astounded that the matter had clarified itself so simply.

I was shortly to leave Turkowice. This time not my mother, but rather my aunt Teodora, came for me. By now the weather was beautiful, but my boils had worsened considerably, I had painful suppurating wounds and was staying in the isolation ward. Again the departure was postponed. I supposed, perhaps, that I would stay there forever, insofar as obstacles were accumulating, yet I was not despondent, I'd grown used to Turkowice, and it's not impossible that I no longer imagined life beyond it and feared everything that would be new. I was not to wait long, though. After some time the next aunt, Maria, came, and she was resolved to take me with her regardless of the circumstances. Luckily I had recovered somewhat and could set out on the journey.

I remember perfectly the day of my departure. It was sunny and sweltering, typical for the height of summer (it was early August). When Maria appeared it was already past noon; she had managed to persuade the Hrubieszów railwayman to engage the trolley and start toward Turkowice. He had set one condition: by dusk at the latest we had to be back in Hrubieszów, because the area continued to be dangerous, especially at night. We had to hurry; the railwayman's condition was justified and couldn't be treated lightly. I didn't have time to say good-bye to everyone or to bring my life in Turkowice to a close. Sister Alojza gave me a school report, signed by herself and by a teacher, a former convent preceptor who had taken up residence there several weeks earlier. The report certified that I had completed the fifth grade, which was an arbitrary claim as likewise an overstatement inspired by goodwill, for after all I hadn't attended school systematically either in Turkowice or in any other place. Had I discovered I'd completed only the third grade, it would have been equally justified—and I wouldn't have been in the least bit surprised.

I hurriedly bade farewell to the nuns and thanked them. Other activities that usually precede setting out on a journey required neither time nor effort. Packing took not even a minute, as I had no things of my own (not even a toothbrush, which during the war had become an unfamiliar object in Turkowice). I was a passenger without baggage. Yet I could not travel without shoes, and in summertime in Turkowice we went about barefoot. Sister Róża found the shoes I'd arrived in a year and a half earlier and which I wore in the winter. I tried to push my sore, and as was to be revealed shortly, too-big feet into them. After some time I managed, but walking in them was difficult. I ran to the trolley barefoot, holding my shoes in my hand. I didn't part with them, as I still supposed that somehow I would squeeze into them, it wasn't proper to go without shoes in the city, and they became the main accessory to my journey.

We set off. The tracks ran through a dense wood. Right away Maria's pocket mirror broke; we wondered whether this was a bad or a good sign. On that severely scorched earth terrible things continued to take place, and there were things to fear. As we approached the area the railwayman had described as especially dangerous, we heard the echoes of shots coming from far away. As he wished, we reached Hrubieszów just as dusk began to gather. The journey's first stage—relatively short, but not free of dangers—was behind us. We were to set out again early in the morning of the following day.

We needed to reach Chełm, whence trains ran to Warsaw. Between that city and Hrubieszów there were no regular connections, we had to seek out an opportunity. Someone told us that a young married couple was going to Chełm by wagon, that they were moving to the west with the intention of settling in the Recovered Territories, and perhaps we could manage to be taken along with them. They accepted us readily. I remember that ride through beautiful surroundings. The road led through forest hillocks, through no longer green meadows, lightly yellowed but still magnificent, fields that enticed the eyes with their many colors. In the light of the intense August sun, it all looked beautiful. I think it was just then, for the first time, that I became enchanted with nature. I gazed at it with a disinterested eye, not fearing that something would unexpectedly attack, destroy, and devour me. The wild and magnificent woods stretching between Turkowice and Hrubieszów had been forbidding—they seemed malevolent, bristling with hostility, aggressive, and ready to expel anyone who recklessly penetrated them—whereas this landscape was open and gentle. Or perhaps it was I who was becoming a different person and was finding inside myself what was needed to perceive and admire nature, I who was becoming someone who, even if only slowly, to a small extent, was liberating himself from fear? Fear precludes the contemplation of nature;

it erodes certain aptitudes and circumscribes possibilities. A hunted animal seeks refuge—and does not reflect upon the potential beauty of its surroundings.

Our traveling companions—and in fact our benefactors, for if not for their wagon, we would have had difficulty getting to Chełm—turned out to be warm and kindhearted people. They must have understood that I was starving, and they constantly offered me something from what they had brought along for their long journey. They didn't need to cajole me; it was my first gorging in many years. Everything they offered me seemed wonderful, and I didn't listen to Maria's warnings that I should be more moderate in devouring these sumptuous country delicacies. I wasn't aware of what could happen when the demands of the stomach, condemned to starvation rations and so little satisfied for so long, would be fulfilled with such appreciable interest. I didn't think of the consequences of my gluttony. Unfortunately these manifested themselves before long. My journey to Warsaw, now by train, took a turn for the wretched; in an unbearably overcrowded compartment, I was given a seat by the window, not, of course, so that I could observe the scenery. We were traveling, after all, by night.

It was already light when we arrived the next morning. We arrived in the Praga district, because trains coming from the east did not reach the left bank of Warsaw at that time. We had to get to Nowogrodzka Street, from there a local narrow-gauge train, known by its prewar acronym EKD, left for Pruszków; we had go on foot because there was no municipal transport. I set off, proudly holding my shoes in my hand—my shoes that were old and ragged and above all uncomfortable since they were too small. I thought it would be better this way, but I was quickly persuaded that walking barefoot through the devastated city was an especially trying task, so onerous as to be unfeasible. Again I tried to force my unhappy feet into the shoes. And these problems left perhaps the greatest impression evoked by my passage through the ruined city. I can't say that I knew Warsaw, but I did remember something of it from my prewar childhood. This and that from September 1939, which we had spent in my aunt Teodora's apartment on Wspólna Street, had imprinted itself. Before my eyes I had the ghetto and some sections of the Aryan Side, although they didn't form a cohesive space—they were rather specific points connected with specific events. For me the scorched and devastated city was a pile of ruins, and I could not treat them as palimpsests from which I could read what had once been in a given place. My attention was mainly absorbed by the growing difficulty of walking, the growing number of blisters on my feet, and the growing pain of each step. Was it far still to Nowogrodzka Street, where the train was, and where I could finally take off my infernal shoes?

In Pruszków I walked barefoot on the road from the station, located just next to the famous psychiatric hospital on Szkolna Street where after the war my family found refuge for a short time in a small block of flats belonging to Burchardt the baker. My mother was waiting for me. And at once she set about washing me. It was an intense scouring, removing the dirt that had amassed not only during the onerous journey, but also across long years. Was it at just this moment that the war and the occupation ended for me?

✤

Misjudeja

Ever since childhood I've been fascinated by words, by strange
and unusual words I heard only rarely, words captivating in
their originality, sometimes peculiar-sounding, sometimes familiar, but most often exotic, words in which I could find nothing I already knew. In my own way, I collected them, like postage
stamps, although I lacked a system for organizing them; in any
case organization wasn't important to me. I felt as if first encounters with words previously unheard expanded my world,
elucidating unfamiliar aspects and qualities—just as stamps
open vistas on distant and unreachable countries, so did words
outline imaginary journeys on which I set forth without inhibi-
tions. For me words were not abstract and ephemeral, but rather
concrete and material; at times it seemed I could hold them in
my hand.

I'm certain I would not have remembered this woman had she
not been connected in my consciousness with a long and odd-
sounding word. I recall that she appeared in Pruszków just after
I had returned from the convent in Turkowice where I had spent
the last phase of the occupation. It was during the period before
we moved to the house my grandfather had built around the turn
of the century, when he was just starting out as a young lumber
merchant, and hence it must have been late summer or early autumn of 1945. I would not have remembered her, because from
my perspective, at least, there was nothing distinctive about her

that would have drawn my attention. Her visit lasted a short time, two hours or perhaps three. She had come to Pruszków wanting to learn the fate of her family from those who had survived; she came in the hope that someone from her family was still living, and when she heard no good news, she asked where they had died, in what circumstances. And, like everyone, she told of her own fate during the occupation, about how she managed to survive, about the terror and suffering. Even though I was barely ten years old, I carried the weight of my own experiences, I bore the hump of the occupation, which I was wholly unable to shed, I listened readily to stories of suffering, death, and escape. In fact nothing else interested me. The occasions were innumerable, such topics were spoken of constantly, it was difficult to speak about anything else. The time of the Holocaust had consummated itself, it had come to an end, yet it still existed in everyone who had survived. This was true all the more so given that only with its end did it become possible to calculate the balance of losses—and thus the silent call of the murdered.

The story of the woman who sought news of her family (before the war they had lived in Pruszków) did not stick in my memory. The woman herself I remember as if through a fog. She was a brunette whose appearance corresponded well to images of Semitic beauty, although to me she appeared old, ruined, and witchlike. But even these fragmented remnants would not have stayed in my memory had my aunt not called her "Misjudeja," thus was she also referred to after her departure. It was one of those previously unheard words that captured my attention, I could not but take note of it. At first I thought this was a peculiar, perhaps even amusing name. And I'd grown used to peculiar women's names when I was around nuns (which was the case not only at Turkowice), and so I remembered then—as I do to this day—Sister Prudencja and Sister Anuncjata, Sister Petronela and Sister Leontyna. "Misjudeja," however, was not really a name. What this woman's name was, I don't know—nor am I ever to find out. At the time I didn't know how to interpret this expression, I certainly didn't associate it with "Jude," a word that often resounded in my ears, even though I didn't know German. Only after some time did I realize that this was actually not one word, that I'd heard this grouping of sounds in a certain way because I didn't know how to separate the component parts. And so I learned that this woman, who to me seemed so old and ugly, had won a Jewish beauty contest shortly before the war and been awarded the title "Miss Judea." I don't know what kind of contest this was; it must have been the counterpart of the competition whose finale was the awarding of the title "Miss Polonia." It's difficult for me, though, to say whether this was a nationwide pageant organized by a Jewish association, or only metropolitan or provincial. But the scope of the contest is of no great significance here. I'm reflecting on something else: during those good times before the war, a young girl was distinguished for something that during the occupation became her curse, radically reducing her chances of survival. For then one could no longer speak of a "beautiful Jewess;" what had become important was that her looks were Semitic, and therefore "bad," and thus while she was in hiding on the Aryan Side, her very features drew danger toward her. The laureate of the Jewish beauty contest found herself in a situation especially drastic during times when dark eyes and an insufficiently straight nose had become a marker determining a person's life or death. Misjudeja was from one of the small towns just outside of Warsaw, perhaps Żyrardów or Grodzisko. I don't know where and how she survived; her aged face lined with deep wrinkles testified to the devastating and severe experiences she had behind her. She didn't find anyone from her family in our town, nor did she learn anything about what had happened to them, surely they were typical, bearing no qualities that would have set them apart: the ephemeral ghetto in Pruszków, the Warsaw Ghetto, and then Umschlagplatz and the gas chambers in Treblinka. Misjudeja never again appeared here (what did she have to look for here?), shortly afterward, it was said, she left Poland.

I also remember other people who, having miraculously survived, appeared in Pruszków. At the time I didn't connect them with Job, but now—for years now—the comparison irresistibly suggests itself. If the survivors were religious, then they believed they were searching for those who had perished "by the breath of God" and were consumed "by the blast of His anger." Yet I think that after what had happened, those who were religious ceased to be so, and to God they could direct only the reproach: "Thou hast made desolate all my company." They became people for whom the morning is as "the shadow of death; for they know the terrors of the shadow of death." In this way do I remember those few survivors who had once been somehow connected to Pruszków, and who came here hoping perhaps to find someone still living or at least learn something about their fate. I remember, too, those few people from Pruszków who settled here again after the war, but only for a short time, typically they left quickly, usually to go abroad. Surely they did so for various reasons, above all to distance themselves from a space that—although inhabited—had become empty for them, for it had been transformed into one vast burial ground. How to live where thy company hast been made desolate!

I remember several such people, even though not all their names have stayed in my memory. I remember those people who for the most part were alone, although they once had families numbering many; each was a solitary creature of misfortune, weighed down by what had taken place. Yet they must not have thought only about the past and those they had lost. They must have also contemplated what to do with themselves in a world that was not and could no longer ever be the authentic world, the world into which they had been born, the world in which— as it undoubtedly had seemed to them at one time—they would live out their lives, perhaps gray and uninteresting, yet in their own way normal, lives vulnerable to dangers and threats, yet certainly not ending in a chamber filled with deadly gas.

So do I recall Wajcer the tailor, who spoke an odd, imperfect Polish. By some miracle he managed to survive, but he was left alone: his whole family had perished. He had to live somehow, and so he returned to his profession, but he gave the impression of someone half out of his mind, someone unable to find a place for himself in a world that had lost all connection with the world that was once his. I recall Pani Kligowa; she, too, had lost everyone and mourned for them, astonished that she in particular remained alive, when she should have perished like the others. Pani Kligowa and Wajcer the tailor were no longer young—or in any case so it seemed to me then, but I don't think I would have been mistaken—yet they became a couple. While they surely did not believe that two ill fortunes joined together would create something new, they must have reasoned that together they could more easily bear their fate. I don't know what shape their life together took or whether they remained together, before long they left Pruszków. I would suppose that they filled much of their time with stories of what had happened to them during the years of the Holocaust, stories preserving their experiences and honoring the dead, but also allowing them to control the pain, to objectify it, and so—at least to some extent—to overcome it. This continual relating of ordeals and experiences became part of the existence of those who survived, had those stories been transcribed or recorded, the most authentic Book of the Holocaust would have come into being, the only one of its kind.

I recall still other people, like Pani Rozenblumowa and her son Olek, who was my age. Like Misjudeja, her looks were Semitic, she was dark, her luxuriant hair was a striking jet black. I'm unable to say much about her, Olek I remember better, I interacted with him on several occasions. Yet he, too, soon left together with his mother, it seems to some place far away, perhaps Australia. The figure of Pan Kenigsztajn, rather short and agitated, still flashes across the screen of my memory. He survived with his wife and two children; for a long time he was in hiding in terrible conditions in a dugout in Podlasie. They too left, and shortly thereafter the news arrived that Pan Kenigsztajn had died suddenly of a heart attack. It was not his good fortune to enjoy postwar life.

I also remember people who, like Misjudeja, appeared in Pruszków for a short time, wanting to find someone they had known before the cataclysm or to learn of someone's fate. Once, unexpectedly, a young man came in a military uniform, he was the son of people my grandparents had known before the war. His parents had perished in the Warsaw Ghetto, but even so he was fortunate, because he found his sister. Fate had thrown him to the East, and he returned to Poland as a soldier in Berling's Army. He didn't want to stay here; he said that as soon as he was demobilized, he would go to Palestine to fight for an independent Jewish state. And I suppose he did, because he didn't appear in Pruszków again. Of all those I've mentioned here, he remains before my eyes as the only one who smiled, as being—despite everything—not so crushed by the weight of the war as those who had lived through that ghastly period at home. He spoke about Russia, not concealing what he thought, as he was far removed from the propagandistic mythology that already then— in late 1945—resounded quite audibly throughout Poland. His story—despite everything—was less intensely dismal than the stories one could hear from Misjudeja or Wajcer the tailor.

My recollections from the first postwar years in Pruszków assume the shapes in which they emerge from my memory, even while forming, at times, their own narratives. I would like to conclude what I might title "Misjudeja's Narrative." No, I will not add anything about her fate in later years, because I know nothing. I'm thinking of those people who, many years after the Holocaust, were still searching, no longer for relatives—for no longer was there a shadow of hope that they had survived—but rather for news of how they perished, where, and in what conditions. Later, many years after the war, when we were already living in Warsaw, a stranger from Chile appeared in Pruszków searching for his Jewish family. No one there was able to tell him anything, but someone suggested that perhaps he could find out something from us. The Chilean engineer had been born in our town in the mid-twenties, but he didn't remember Poland—as a child, he had emigrated with his family to the other side of the globe. His Polish was less than proficient, and he spoke with a strange accent, intermixing what must have been smatterings of Spanish and Yiddish. Still he was able to communicate without problems. He inquired about the fate of his aunts, uncles, and cousins, he mentioned their names and occupations and read their prewar addresses from a piece of paper—and in this way reconstructed a world that he himself had not known and was now never to know. He reconstructed it as if he had not anticipated that all had been entirely lost, as if he had hoped suddenly to hear that even one of his relatives remained alive. Yet he heard nothing like this. My mother recalled some of the names he mentioned, she knew that such people had lived in Pruszków before the war. But what could she say of their fates? She knew no concrete details and could only describe a path: first the ephemeral ghetto in Pruszków, then the Warsaw Ghetto, Umschlagplatz, and the gas chambers of Treblinka. The fates of the condemned were schematic, the privilege of an individual death had been taken from them as well.

I remember that the engineer from Chile, who had been born in Pruszków, stayed in our house for another hour or two after he learned that he would learn nothing. The conversation went on about neutral subjects, filling up time, avoiding what was significant. I entertained his wife, who had no connection to Poland, with small talk in French. This conversation took place almost twenty years after the Holocaust, yet the questions of our unexpected guest rendered it once more piercingly present, as present as it had been when Misjudeja appeared just after the war ended. Time takes away hope, but leaves wounds unhealed.

It Was I Who Killed Jesus

It was surely not an especially important episode in my already fairly long life, and I would have every reason to count it among those episodes of my childhood to which one ascribes no weight, or simply to forget that it happened. Things turned out otherwise. The episode was preserved in my consciousness, it returned to me at various times and in various situations, as if it concealed a deeper meaning or had acquired symbolic significance. In comparison with what had befallen me earlier, this incident from school is almost a trifle, for in no way was my life threatened, it was rather a small instance of the unpleasantness to which one is perpetually vulnerable. I realize this, and yet still cannot resist the temptation to relate it, and so purge it from myself, and perhaps in this way finally bring the matter to a close.

The whole story was initiated by a boy in my class who was so remote from me and so poorly inscribed in my memory that even today, years later, I can't really call him a classmate. His last name was Szymański; I'm unable to recall his first name. I do remember what he looked like: though no athlete, he distinguished himself by his mass. I see clearly and vividly his exceptionally pale crop of hair, almost the color of an albino's, and a distinctively elongated face, giving the impression of a blockhead, oddly pointed and angular. And his eyes: pale blue, washed out, as if someone had thrown whitener into their natural color. He was a poor student, one of the worst in the class. Yet I, too, was

147

far from the best—I dithered around somewhere near the bottom, rarely getting better than adequate grades, which had to satisfy me at the time. Szymański's attitude toward me, ever more malevolent, did not emerge then from the complexes of a poor student who cannot stand a better one. Had that been the case, he would have had much more fitting targets of hatred among our class, and could have vented his aggression on them. The issue was something else.

He knew of my origins, everyone did. My family, settled in Pruszków since time immemorial, was well known. He knew, even though I myself didn't stand out in any way; I even attended religion classes, since my parents, still carrying within themselves the fear from the occupation years, decided that being safe meant blending into the surroundings, they didn't want to expose me to hostility or new persecutions. And what happened was connected to the lessons taught by Father Franciszek B. in our school. I don't know whether Szymański was especially religious—I would have my doubts—but he did live in a world of images shaped by a peculiarly conceptualized religiosity, a religiosity in which love for one's neighbor played an incomparably lesser role than did hatred toward others, such as pagans, heretics, and Jews. Szymański did not conceal his hatred for me, he displayed it on various occasions and was demonstrative in his disgust, even though I hadn't offended him in any direct way. I avoided him, as he inspired dread and reminded me of what had happened so recently. My very existence irritated him, he may have regarded it as scandalous. In his mouth the word "Jew" directed at me was the worst invective, it was meant as the most abominable condemnation. But he didn't limit himself to words. On a certain occasion he announced that on the last day of school, he would put me in my place and deliver to me the appropriate punishment. I was guilty of nothing toward him, and so he had no reason to punish me, yet the issue here was not really about me or about him, the scale of the charges was significantly greater. Szymański wanted to dispense justice for a great crime: the Jews had murdered Jesus. All of them bore responsibility for deicide. I, too, had taken part in this, I, too, had killed Jesus—and I had done this personally, with my own hands.

At that time, in the first years after the occupation, I was riddled with anxiety, unable to liberate myself from the ghastly experiences and dread that lived inside me and defined my relationship to the world. Still, I wasn't worried by this proclamation, and I didn't take it seriously. I saw no cause for alarm; Szymański had jostled me and hurled abuse on me many times, yet I hadn't expected that he would actually indicate the day of punishment and seriously contemplate its execution. I was quickly to learn that he was not just tossing words into the air. After all, he had no right to relinquish so pious an intention, he had to teach Jesus's murderer a lesson.

It was one of the last days of June 1947, sunny, and very hot. The ceremony of distributing report cards had concluded around noon, and seventh grade was now happily behind me. I was in an exceptionally good mood. I'd passed, although my modest, barely average grades didn't speak well of either my abilities or my diligence. I was glad that at least for two months I wouldn't have to look at the school, which I honestly couldn't stand, or at my classmates, none of whom had become my friend. And as far as Szymański was concerned, I supposed that his declaration was just the prank of a boy who, at the end of the school year, wanted to thoroughly intimidate me one more time.

Cheerful, smiling, content, I was on my way home. Halfway down the road, just next to the block of flats where Cegielski's bakery, well known in our neighborhood, was located, before the thoroughfare dividing May 3rd Street into two unequal parts (the viaduct wasn't there at the time, it was built much later), Szymański emerged with another boy I didn't know. Initially I didn't pay him any attention; I supposed it was a chance meeting, which after all isn't uncommon in a small town, especially on a day when schoolchildren were returning home to boast of their grades to their families. It was only after a moment that I grasped the extent of my error. Szymański was a serious youth who didn't utter words in vain. Aided by his companion, he im-

mediately set to work. These two peers of mine fell upon me in
the usual way, showering me with blows from all sides, doubtlessly convinced that they acted from noble intentions and on behalf of a noble aim, for they were delivering punishment for my
crime. After all it was I who had killed Jesus; in this matter,
Szymański (and surely also his companion, called upon to assist)
harbored no doubts.

In shock, I didn't even think of defending myself, instead I
cringed. In such situations a person instinctively assumes that
the lesser the surface of the body exposed to blows, the lesser the
pain. I'm unable today to reconstruct reliably what I felt then;
yet I do know that it was one of those situations in which I felt
that my world was collapsing, that something was happening to
deprive the world of sense and to direct it in its entirety against
me. It was a great shock, not only in a strictly physical sense—
in total I received only a few blows and would surely have received more had an unknown man not come to my defense and
driven away the assailants—but also in a deeper sense, because
that sudden attack allowed me to see, or so I thought, that I
would always be alienated, that neither in Pruszków nor anywhere else would I ever find a place for myself. I felt the shock as
an extension of the occupation, which I still carried inside myself, I hadn't forgotten my experiences, and as I matured, I grew
ever more aware of them. At once I understood that Szymański
was not beating me because we had some kind of account to
settle from school, or because he was taking revenge for something I actually did. This was not the usual vagary of a boy my
age who, unable to control the aggression inside him, lashes out
at someone he doesn't like for whatever reason, or someone arbitrary who happens to appear. He was dispensing justice, acting
from higher motives. After all, I was a God-killer.

I had no doubts as to how this idea had come into Szymański's
head. Perhaps he'd been acquainted with it earlier, but he heard
this idea incessantly at the religion lessons conducted by Father
Franciszek B., and he concretized it and related it to me, because
I was within his reach. Citing the authority of the Church and

the principles of faith, Father Franciszek B. taught that all Jews always and everywhere were responsible for the crucifixion—all Jews without exception, regardless of where and when they lived—and that this was an unalterable fact. I grasped quickly that this ecclesiastic had played his part in what had happened to me, and that the attack was the direct consequence of his teachings. I'm not claiming, of course, that he ordered Szymański to beat me for belonging to the accursed and loathsome tribe of God-killers, but in certain instances formulating instructions and issuing orders, per se, is unnecessary: the conclusions emerge on their own. The slow-witted and simpleminded Szymański revealed himself to be a sharp pupil.

The religion lessons taught by Father Franciszek B. were sessions of hatred. He represented that most peculiar kind of Christianity in which the Sermon on the Mount is unworthy of mention, and in which love for one's neighbor—or in any case love for a neighbor whom one dislikes for some reason—is discarded. Father Franciszek B., a tall, broad-shouldered, gray-haired man, his youth already long behind him, was undoubtedly an absorbing figure. I know much about him, because he enjoyed talking about himself during class; this topic evidently did not bore him, and his discussions of it were unhindered by the youth of his audience. Above all he did not conceal his pride at having been descended from good heraldic nobility and at bearing a surname with traditions. Unfortunately, his family, long settled in distant eastern borderlands, had become impoverished; had material conditions permitted him an education, he would not have been inclined toward the seminary. He didn't conceal that poverty had determined his calling, that he had joined the clergy in the absence of another choice. With bewildering frankness he confessed that he would have preferred to become a physician or an attorney. At the time when I listened as he imparted these secrets, I didn't understand what I see today from the perspective of distance: Father Franciszek B. was constantly playing out the drama of his unsuccessful existence, constantly wrestling with it, unable to overcome it, and he initiated the students at this

school (which in accordance with custom was still named after
Piłsudski) in his secrets. He was, with complete certainty, a
deeply unhappy person. And without any qualms he made it understood that the status of a priest failed to bring him any great satisfaction. His ped-
agogical obligations in particular wearied him, apart perhaps
from one: he very much enjoyed the presence of teenage girls
in the class. Only with them did he feel his calling, and he conducted the lessons as if he noticed them alone (the boys were an
uninteresting, anonymous mass, whose existence he barely perceived). He was partial to the developed and the pretty ones, he
stroked and caressed them and asked them to sit close to him. I
don't know if he especially liked Lolitas, or if this was simply the
only kind of contact with femininity available to him. I don't
know nor do I want to search for the answer; I mention this only
because it, too, says something about Father Franciszek B. I won't
pursue this theme, as it has very little directly to do with what
happened to me on the last day of school near the red brick building housing the bakery, which at that time of year sold delicious
berry pastries. Yet much of what transpired at his lessons did
bear some relation to this event.

It was clear that Father Franciszek B. was not predisposed toward conducting systematic lessons. He filled the time between
bells with any old thing, or tried to set up a situation that allowed him to sit passively, not even feigning interest in what was
going on in the classroom (so long as there was not excessive
noise!), or digressing on the most varied topics. That said, many
of the teachings imparted in his class could have inspired Szymański to see me as a criminal guilty of deicide. The Jewish motif recurred ceaselessly.

Father Franciszek B. could sit idly only when he had instructed the pupils to read some text aloud. He chose a didactic
thriller, a novel translated from French and published before the
war by one of the publishing houses connected to the Church. It
told the story of a young man who had come from a good, devout Catholic family, but who rebelled against his family, aban-

doned his faith, and became an evildoer serving the Jews and the Masons. We read that novel in excerpts, most likely for the whole school year. Unfortunately I don't know who the author was, nor do I remember the title, and so cannot go back to it today; and I would do this readily so as to recall the exquisite spiritual nourishment Father Franciszek B. fed his charges. He treated that story about the young man who expelled God from his heart and became a ruffian as a morality tale—and every so often he would explicate its moral significance, providing relevant teachings. In particular he warned us against the Jews: he who goes down evil paths becomes a servant of the Jews, and this begets the greatest evil in the world and dooms him to eternal condemnation. In the year 1946 or 1947, Father Franciszek B. had no doubts as to the identity of the greatest menace in the world, from whose influence the youth must be guarded. Jews were an obsessively recurring theme of many lessons; in his formulation they comprised a universal symbol of evil, and when he spoke of them, a surprising vigor emerged in him, such as tended to be lacking when he meditated on the sacred truths. I could not help but notice that this issue affected him personally and that he was not merely evoking it in order to fill up the school's obligatory hours of instruction.

Father Franciszek B. continually insisted that the Jews had murdered Jesus—not only those in ancient Palestine who had demanded the crucifixion, but all of them, including the Jews alive today. For Jews were unchanging by their very nature. They yielded not to the influence of time, nor did they know evolution, they had always thirsted for blood—at one time the blood of Jesus, and later that of Christian children, whom they murdered because they needed the blood to prepare matzo. Ritual murder was a permanent motif of Father Franciszek B.'s lectures, and he returned to it continually, as if the very act of speaking about this cruelty enacted by God-killers gave him particular pleasure, as if the vision of innocent, pious babes slaughtered by *peyes*-wearing, bloodthirsty evildoers afforded him a sensual and sadistic satisfaction. He would mention all too frequently a certain Beilis, who was said to have committed ritual murder and who for that crime had justly been put before the court in Kiev. Of course the Beilis case was not isolated, it only became the most renowned because the criminals did not succeed in concealing it from Christian opinion. Thus he was wont to speak in the plural of "Beilises," treating the word as if it related in a self-evident way to the whole loathsome Jewish nation. In essence I don't wonder that Szymański, after listening many times to this kind of teaching, would be seized with a desire to deliver justice to someone whom he judged to represent that nation. In proceeding to attack me on the day that report cards were distributed, he was beating a concrete person, but in truth this was not his point. He was delivering justice to the representative of a species. And when he resolved to do this, he was simply drawing practical conclusions from what he had heard from Father Franciszek B. True, Father Franciszek B.'s teachings included no calls to action, yet sometimes explicit appeals are not required for the word to be made flesh, especially when the students are favorably disposed to what the teacher is saying.

Needless to say, I did not belong to those favorably disposed. I couldn't stand Father Franciszek B.'s lessons. Even though I sat there with my shoulders hunched, in mouselike quiet, I knew that they were directed against me as well. My ordeals remained in my freshest memory; I had found myself inside a world sentenced to annihilation, and thus everything he said on this subject particularly mattered to me, even if only because this catastrophe was—and remains to this day—the most important experience of my life. In general Father Franciszek B. behaved as if he hadn't noticed the Holocaust at all, as if he had heard nothing about it, as if the fact that millions of people had disappeared from the earth he walked on—people whom for various reasons he scorned, but whose existence he could not question—had failed to capture his attention. From time to time, however, he did refer to the recent years of the occupation, and on these occasions he said that the Jews had met with nothing more than a just punishment for the murder of Jesus. (But were the accounts now settled?) And once it came to pass that he said something still more terrifying. While acknowledging that Hitler was terrible because he had persecuted the Polish nation, he maintained that Hitler did have one merit: he had taken care of the Jewish question on our behalf (or in our stead). I don't remember how I reacted to Father Franciszek B.'s dictum, I must have fallen still more deeply into myself and become more intensely terrified than usual, because I understood that he had transgressed a certain boundary and was candidly praising a crime.

In the decades that followed I was twice to encounter an opinion of this sort—and on each occasion I thought those words were a verdict on me as well, even though most of those who thought this way were expressing their approbation for the annihilation of a collectivity, doubtlessly forgetting that the collectivity was composed of individuals. I don't imagine that even Father Franciszek B., so consistent in unfolding his theology of hatred, listened joyfully to news of the murder of concrete persons, despite their belonging to the "Beilises." And when I heard for the last time those words voiced in a train compartment by an elegant and, in all probability, not poorly educated gentleman, who was unaware that he was conversing with someone for whom they had particular meaning, I had the thought that it was, to all intents and purposes, tactlessness on my part that I had survived.

I've written at length about Father Franciszek B., although I wanted to tell the story of what happened on the street, of how I was beaten on the last day of school. But I don't consider this account of a man who elicited my distaste virtually from the first encounter as a digression, for even at the time I realized that it was he who bore responsibility for that episode, if only because he taught hatred in the sublimity of his sacerdotal authority. My family harbored no doubts; while no one knew Father Franciszek B. personally, his persona emerged from what I would tell them about school, and I couldn't help but mention the peculiar teachings he imparted to his students. I related at once what had befallen me—after all, it was evident from the state in which I returned that something dreadful had occurred.

Getting home was not easy. I reacted to the unexpected assault with uncontrollable, hysterical tears. I was unable to stop them, violent sobbing overcame me, and I began to wail. My behavior couldn't go unobserved by passersby, all the more so due to its vivid contrast with the cheerfulness of the other children, who were happy that the school year had ended. I overheard the comments of two girls I didn't know, who said that I was crying because I hadn't passed. On such a day it was the simplest explanation, it suggested itself. I knew this, but I was unable to set things straight and shout that I was crying for a completely different reason, that I was crying because a great and undeserved injury had been done to me. For after all I knew that I had not killed Jesus, I was astounded that such a thought could have come into someone's head. And the supposition that I had failed intensified my pain, and I felt doubly humiliated.

And thus the episode concluded. That is, it concluded as a concrete event, since seen from another perspective, it endured in me for years, defining my behavior and my ways of seeing the world. As a result of it my fear of people, which had reached its peak during the occupation and had been slowly receding in the postwar years, grew in me anew. Once again I became convinced, and palpably so, that anyone could direct absurd grudges at me, could accuse me of offenses having no basis in myself or in the real world, and that these were not merely empty words but would be followed by actions. Again I felt threatened and alienated. For some time I was afraid to leave the house; inside its walls I found refuge, I felt safer there than I did in any other place.

This episode, which from the beginning I associated with the teachings imparted by Father Franciszek B., had still other consequences. I felt him to be so repugnant a figure that he inclined me to a distaste—or at least a distrust—toward the clergy in general. My contact with him foreordained my relatively easy submission to the anticlerical propaganda that flourished lavishly in a postwar Poland undergoing accelerated communization. It seemed to me that behind each cassock lurked his figure. Aside from brief and chance encounters, devoid of any consequence, I had little contact with men of the cloth in my postwar life. At the lyceum I attended religion was taught by two priests in succession. They differed fundamentally from Father Franciszek B. They treated their tasks seriously, presented biblical history and the sacred truths in an interesting manner, and related to their students amiably. I had no reason to complain about them, and yet I was mistrustful, I worried that something would suddenly cause the differences to be revealed as superficial, and that again I would hear words of hatred and glimpse a new embodiment of Father Franciszek B. So deeply had he settled in my consciousness that for some time I almost forgot about the people to whom I owe my life: the wonderful Mother Superior from Turkowice, the kind and solicitous Sister Róża, and finally the remarkable Father Stanisław Bajka, the Jesuit who was the chaplain in Turkowice during the occupation years and who meant so much to all of us.

On various occasions I was reminded of Father Franciszek B. (he died, if I'm not mistaken, in the second half of the fifties, when he was well past seventy). Once it happened quite unexpectedly, while I was reading. In a certain article by Father Tischner I came across a sentence particularly resonant, it seems to me, with respect to the case I'm concerned with here: "In my life I have not met anyone who has lost faith after reading Marx and Lenin, yet I have met many who have lost faith after meeting with their own parish priest." I think that Father Franciszek B. turned at least those like myself away from the clergy and the Church more effectively than the most zealous agitator from the Society of Atheists and Freethinkers. He turned me away—and not only for a short time.

✿

Books I Didn't Read in My Youth

Some years ago I was asked by a renowned Kraków literary publication to write about books I had read during my childhood. I declined, because for the most part I would have had to deal not with books, but with why I hadn't read them, and this naturally would have conflicted with the concept of the series. Yet this was not the primary issue for me; at the time I wasn't yet psychologically prepared to write for publication about things connected with the most intimate aspects of my biography. If I spoke about these experiences at all, it was only to a small number of people from my closest circle—and this I did only rarely and timidly. I knew that my counternarrative about what I hadn't read when I was young would by necessity not concern books. That I have gaps in this realm I realized long ago, years before I received that invitation, for when my classmates—those my age and a bit older—sentimentally recalled their early reading material, I was condemned to silence, having nothing about which to speak. All that they recalled was unfamiliar to me, at best I had heard of a few things second- or third-hand. I have to confess that I listened with some jealousy to their recollections, I thought of what had passed me by in childhood. Surely I, too, would have devoured with flushed cheeks the tales of wonderful adventures in the Wild West.

When the war broke out, I was not yet five years old; during the good times—which for decades afterward would be nostalgically defined by the words "before the war"—I didn't yet know how to read. I had looked at some picture books; one has stayed in my memory. When the book was opened, the letters, appropriately cut out and pasted onto thick cardboard pages, stood up. This book must have been my first alphabet lesson, and I must have been made to read the short poem, given that I remember the last sentence: "W stood upon its head, pretending to be M instead." Only years later did I learn that its author was Tuwim. But even at that time I had already heard this name, for I was read "The Locomotive," and the agglomeration of words "*lokomotywa Tuwima*" sounded like part of a poem—this was among his onomatopoeic effects, and perhaps just for this reason I remembered it. To a child, especially a young child, the names of authors are unimportant. And so I didn't know who had written the fairy tale I was captivated by, about the wonderful march of the animals, which at a certain moment fell apart, all growing terrified when a cockroach emerged from behind a bush and menacingly moved its tendrils. I was struck by the ridiculousness of the situation: large and mighty animals, among them splendid and majestic lions, terrified by a smallish insect. Only decades later did I find out that this work by Kornei Chukovskii, which with a child's naïveté I had understood literally, was an example of Aesopian language, and the hideous tendriled cockroach was a bloodthirsty dictator, one of the greatest criminals in human history. A side effect of having taken Chukovskii's fairy tale to heart was a fear of cockroaches, linked to an irrational disgust that has stayed with me to this day.

I don't remember when or how I learned to read; it came to me easily, quickly, without problems. The war broke out, and I wasn't going to school for obvious reasons; I think I acquired that ability as early as the first months of the war. I left the ranks of juvenile illiterates, yet I don't remember reading anything during that time. The adults, terrified by what had occurred, unadapted to the new situation and, above all, to the threats that were intensifying every day, had more important and absorbing activities than supplying me with reading material. Perhaps I did read something, only nothing has stayed in my memory; perhaps I didn't come across anything that made an impression on me, it's not impossible that by then it was not stories in books but rather what I saw in the world around me that made an impression. Somewhat later, in the ghetto, when I was attending Panna Julia and Pani Bronisława's lessons, I became enthusiastic about books. This happened, I think, a short time before the commencement of transports to Treblinka. During this period the ghetto was still "normal," there was some kind of lending library for children, and my father signed me up. I read two novels, which have become lodged in my memory—children's versions of *Robinson Crusoe* and *Gulliver's Travels*. Most likely it ended with that, as then the most dreadful stage began—transports, liquidation. Once again I had no books within reach; perhaps I forgot about the existence of books in general. I was aware that at every moment death stood at the threshold, rapping on the door. The threat of the transport to Treblinka grew more real from day to day, I lived in intensifying fear, and this was not conducive to reading. When people are being killed all around, reading isn't effective in killing time.

Between the onset of the initial season of journeys to Treblinka and our escape from the ghetto, I did have some books, although only one of them was strictly speaking for reading. I remember a thick volume of Grimm's fairy tales, with illustrations, in a red, very shabby cover; it was in wretched condition, falling apart, although it may well have once been a solidly and attractively produced book. I must have reached for it, as I had all too much free time, I didn't leave the room where we were living. Children were as vulnerable to danger as adults, perhaps even more so (if any kind of gradation is befitting here), since their lives were without justification, even such justification as might warrant a delay in the journey to the gas chambers. The Germans acted logically and rationally: insofar as they had resolved to wipe out a whole society from the surface of the earth, they had to murder mercilessly the youngest as well so that the society would have no chance of rebirth. I didn't go out, with the exception of nearby spots serving as hiding places because they seemed safer. Two further volumes had much greater meaning for me than that collection of fairy tales. The first was a fat chess tome containing descriptions of famous matches. I didn't master all of its riches, but rather dwelled on select matches, although I no longer know according to what system; someone might have pointed out to me which ones would be comprehensible, possibly interesting to me. Nor do I know where that book came from or who gave it to me, although I do remember what it looked like. It was printed on very thin paper—it must have been parchment paper—and the much-frayed cover was dirty gray, the color of things old, heavily used, tattered. It was my great treasure.

My second treasure was an enormous German atlas, most likely originating from the period before Hitler. Its format was large; it weighed several kilograms, and I would spread it out on the floor and look at the world. Naturally I couldn't understand the commentaries and legends, but just looking at the maps was enough for me, it inspired fantasies and dreams of what was far away ("far away," after all, often meant "beyond the walls"). I learned a great deal thanks to those maps. The atlas was needed by the adults as well, they would check the location of the front, in the incessant hope that one day those places would be quite close. However during the times I'm speaking of now, this hope was in vain, the lines where the battles were being waged were desperately far away. Polish localities, too, were the objects of searches in this atlas. At a certain moment the news spread that the Germans intended to liquidate the Warsaw Ghetto, transport the remainder of its inhabitants who were still alive to Poniatowa, and put them to work there. Where was Poniatowa? I recognized that these concrete pieces of information the adults wished to acquire from the monumental atlas were important, that they concerned things on which my life, too, depended; yet despite this, for me the atlas was something else entirely. Today I would describe it as a domain of pure art, its own kind of conjurer of fantasies and images so alluring to an eight-year-old ensconced in the reality of the ghetto. Getting out from behind the walls meant parting with those two beloved books. I understood that in fleeing we were trying to save our lives. I regretted leaving the books, but I was not despondent, perhaps because by then I realized that the loss of even the most valuable things was not worth crying over. And today I know this with complete certainty—it is, I think, one of the lessons carried from childhood. Nothing took the place of those books for me once we were on the Aryan Side, I lost all contact with the printed word. During my life of homelessness I didn't have access to books, and I might have altogether forgotten that they were needed for anything.

When we were hiding in the village, in R., I had a lot of time, which I spent on nothing. It's possible that had there been something to read, I would have taken an interest in it, but nothing of the sort was within reach. In Pani W.'s home there was at least one book, a romance novel published in the interwar years. I started to read it, and I remember how it began: it's either autumn or winter, a young man comes to the manor, he sets out on a stroll around the garden with a young lady, and they engage in refined conversation. I managed to get through only a dozen or so pages when the mistress of the house energetically interceded, chastising my mother for allowing me to read adult books. "He'll grow up conceited and affected," she pronounced. After a short while she added, "Wacek doesn't read such books." Wacek was her son, older than I by eight or nine years. It's true he didn't read such books, as he didn't read anything at all. He was interested exclusively in pigeons, a pair of which he was enthusiastically raising. That romance novel, perhaps written by Rodziewiczówna or another equally respectable authoress, was taken from me. My attempt at reading was thwarted, and I didn't seek out books for quite a long time. The circumstances were not propitious, the possibility nonexistent, but neither did I manifest any desire.

In Turkowice I didn't become acquainted with a single book,

although I could have had I tried; there was a small library in the convent, but it didn't occur to me to take an interest in it. The library was dominated by religious books, biographies of saints, stories of miracles, and didactic and morality tales of various kinds. But it was not the contents of that library which fore-judged my apathy, especially given that, at the time, those sto-ries contained everything needed to hold my interest. Besides there were also a few items of a different nature. My utter in-ability to read was rather the result of having fallen into a stupor so thorough that I could do little more than sit, passive and un-reflective, on a hard wooden bench.

At just such moments I could observe how a certain classmate was passionately devoting himself to reading, how he devoured one work and not only came back to it over and over again, but further lived through it, forgetting what was around him. His name was Staszek. He was seriously ill, his legs afflicted with deep, leaking wounds, impossible to cure amid the conditions in Turkowice. The bandages were changed, but this was of little help; the disease invaded his body with ever greater intensity. His calves looked ghastly. He was in pain, which must have intensi-fied when he walked, and so he avoided walking. He sat and read. He read *The Trilogy*. The small library was located in the priest's chamber, and once or twice a week at a specified time we could borrow books. A voracious reader, Staszek couldn't wait for that moment—he wanted to keep reading, and when he reached the end, he would begin again—and so he read Sienkiewicz's great trilogy several times. But this was not only reading, it was a way of life; Staszek identified with the heroes, experienced every-thing that befell them, treated their adventures as his own, and perhaps thanks to this, overcame his own wretched situation and entered another, more compelling world. He enjoyed talking to his classmates about it—he did so as if relating experiences that he himself had undergone. This passionate devouring of a book, and moreover a secular book, disconcerted the nuns, who feared it was drawing him away from spiritual matters and more gen-erally guiding him in an inauspicious direction. While Sienkiewicz, to be sure, may have been a great Polish and Catholic writer, he nonetheless could not be equated with authors who conferred religious teachings. Apparently the nuns considered prohibiting him from incessantly reading *The Trilogy*, but most likely it didn't come to that. He continued to devour it—it was, unless I'm mistaken, the only book he liked to read. Everything else seemed boring to him.

I don't know how his fate played out, whether in his adult life, he confined his reading to Sienkiewicz. I didn't follow in his footsteps, in those times I read nothing. I became acquainted with *The Trilogy* only many years later, as a university student required for the exam to produce evidence of familiarity with Polish literature of the second half of the nineteenth century, and so for me it was obligatory reading material. It provided me with none of these wonderful, captivating experiences, I was no longer capable of youthful fascination, in the realm of literature I was drawn elsewhere. Nor did I ever seek out children's literature outside of the Polish literary canon. I didn't pore over the novels of Karl May, and I'm surely never to do that now.

In the first years after the war I read almost nothing. People tried to interest me in one thing or another, but I felt no inclination toward sitting down with books. Not even because books bored me or because I preferred to spend my time in another way—rather, I continued to be spiritless and indifferent, and rarely left the apartment if it was not a necessity. Most of the books read by twelve- or thirteen-year-olds seemed silly to me and above all inconsequential. They didn't relate to my experiences, they corresponded to nothing that had befallen me, and they couldn't serve to overcome my accumulated, still vivid memories. These books were barren for me from the outset. However I did readily seek out varied accounts of the occupation years, I threw myself into everything of that kind that fell into my hands. I remember reading Michał Rusinek's *From the Barricade in the Valley of Hunger,* Gustaw Morcinek's *Letters from under the Mulberry Trees,* and Krystyna Nowakowska's *My Battle for Life.* Titles such as *Smoke over Birkenau* or *I Survived Auschwitz* held a particular attraction for me. Only such literature seemed worthy of my interest, nothing else bore comparison. These books served not as an escape into a world of fantasy; on the contrary, they fixed me inside a world from which I was unable to extricate myself. In one form or another they conjured up what had been the most momentous experience of my life and spoke of events I could treat as analogous or similar to what had been my own fate. Other books seemed trivial to me, I found in them nothing compelling.

There was one exception, however. From the first years after the war I delighted in studying the *Gutenberg Encyclopedia*. It had miraculously survived from my aunt Teodora's prewar library and remained in the house until her move to Warsaw; afterward my father purchased that encyclopedia for me in a used bookstore, and in this way it became my own, I still have and use it. For several years it was the thing I most loved to read; I could spend morning until evening bent over the hard, dark-green covered volumes of that prewar encyclopedia. Today I remember those hours as the most pleasurable in all of my postwar childhood. I was drawn to the encyclopedia above all because it offered concrete knowledge, it spoke of things tangible and confirmed, and moreover did not demand what books of an uninterrupted structure require, that is, the gift of concentration. I didn't read the encyclopedia in the proper order but rather jumped across pages and volumes from one entry to another. I didn't adhere to any principle, my choices were most often arbitrary. So it was until a certain moment, when certain words, names, facts, and topics began to interest me more and more, and this curiosity on the whole then guided my choices—which does not mean I forsook all that fell beyond this sphere. My reading continued to be grasping, rapacious, and untended. That it was not mandatory also belonged among its merits; it provided a knowledge different from the knowledge I acquired in school, which seemed uninteresting and to which I was most often indifferent. My daily immersion in the encyclopedia was, I think, an important agent in my mental and emotional withdrawal from the black seasons;

it comprised a stage, surely far-reaching, in my adaptation to a world which, if not normal, then in any case was common and quotidian, a world in which the most horrific dangers were not emerging from behind each corner at every moment.

As I approached my fifteenth birthday I became a normal reader. No longer did I confine myself to the encyclopedia and to accounts of what was recent and unforgettable. I began to take advantage of Pruszków's town library, well run and abounding in interesting books, including those published before the war. One of Victor Hugo's novels fell into my hands—and fascinated me. I threw myself upon his other works; perhaps it was because stories of various cruelties played so crucial a role in them that I was so responsive. In certain respects they corresponded to what had become my own experience. Yet within a short time I ceased to confine myself to works by this author and began to read avidly the novels of other classic authors, both domestic and foreign, unquestionably intended for adults. That, however, is not the subject of this story.

✿

"Germans Are People, Too"

It was my first vacation by the sea. I went to Międzyzdroje with my father. We stayed in a modest boardinghouse. The room, which must once have served as a parlor, was dilapidated, as was the whole house; like a waiting room at a dentist's office, the room was full of stacks of old papers and periodicals. I looked through them. By that time my not-reading stage was behind me and I was drawn to every printed word; I rummaged through a heap of newspapers, my gaze pausing on this or that. At a certain moment I came upon a shabby page (it was immediately evident that it was an old issue) of the weekly *Odrodzenie*. I'm uncertain whether that title meant something to me, or whether it was my first encounter with that well-known publication, at that time I didn't yet read the literary press. And on the first page I saw, printed in large letters, the sentence: "Germans are people." I figured out that it was an excerpt of a play by Leon Krucz-kowski. Years later, while preparing to write this memoir, I confirmed that this excerpt appeared in the 20 March 1949 issue, and so made its way into my hands several months later. The weekly didn't interest me, though, nor did the play or the author. I was stunned by the sentence "Germans are people." I was stunned and indignant; I didn't know that it was a modernized citation from *Konrad Wallenrod*. I was extremely stunned and indignant, because it questioned my deepest convictions; I absorbed it as an internal contradiction, as if someone had said, "beasts are people." Some few years after the Holocaust, I couldn't at all conceive of such a sentence coming from someone's pen. If I had read that Germans were criminals, villains, butchers, barbarians, or murderers, I wouldn't have stopped to reflect at all; I would have regarded such a sentence as expressing an irrefutable truth and I wouldn't have remembered it. After all, one doesn't remember phrases that express and confirm the obvious. The title from *Odrodzenie* fixed itself forcefully in my consciousness because it countered the experiences I had taken away from the occupation, and I was repulsed by it.

My image of Germans—or rather my image of a German, since the whole nation was embodied in an individual and what that individual did—was extremely straightforward: at any given moment he seeks to murder me, you, someone else. And he will carry out this desire without fail the moment you fall into his hands. He is a criminal with a single goal—killing people such as me and many others. To be sure, this image didn't take shape immediately; it acquired its content as the Final Solution progressed from the realm of planning to the sphere of realization, as I saw what was happening and grew certain that any encounter I would have with a German would mean inescapable death. This was an unquestioned truth during the time of the Holocaust, and even a child could not but be aware of it. I grasped it quickly; lessons of this kind, resulting from fear and unmediated experience, are assimilated instantaneously. Nothing had happened or could happen that would have inclined me, several years after the war, to consign that lesson to oblivion. The teachings drawn from it could not but raise questions the moment when I saw that sentence printed in large type in *Odrodzenie*.

Even though this image did not take shape at once, I knew, almost from the war's very beginning, that a German was someone to be feared. Perhaps I was not entirely conscious of this in September of 1939. I lived through the siege of Warsaw, in the very center of the city, on Wspólna Street. It was a terrifying experience, at different times of night and day we descended into the cellar, as bombs fell nearby. One struck just next to us, yet despite all of that, this was still not it. Perhaps I was too young to absorb the danger of the situation, yet of one thing I am certain: at that time, a German was in some sense a distant and somewhat mysterious enemy, insofar as the pilots hurling bombs on the besieged city were not themselves visible.

"A German" materialized very quickly. I encountered my first act of terror just after the defeat, in autumn 1939, even before the resettlement to the ghetto. At that time a large part of my family had gathered at my grandparents' home in Pruszków. One afternoon a truck arrived with a team of people headed by the gendarme Rothimmel to requisition my grandparents' bedroom furniture. From the moment the invaders arrived that gendarme was the terror of the town—and for me the first embodiment of a German. He was tall, and he shouted most often in German, although supposedly he knew Polish quite well because (so the rumors went) he was from Silesia. We didn't then foresee what the occupation would mean; that men appeared to unceremoniously carry away beds and night tables was doubtlessly a shock. For me it was an important experience: I witnessed German lawlessness for the first time, and I would remember it— together with the shouting of the gendarme—well. Today, though, I'm thinking of something else. The furniture from my grandparents' bedroom—surely solid, bourgeois, but otherwise not particularly special—was needed for accommodations being prepared in Pruszków for a Nazi official. It's striking that he was not repulsed by contact with objects taken from Jews, contaminated by their very touch. I thought about this in particular recently, after seeing at Zachęta an exhibit of photographs depicting the fate of Polish Jews, which showed German soldiers burning the beds taken from Jewish apartments as nests of filth, insects, and pestilence.

The gendarme was a well-known figure in our small town. Later it would be difficult to speak of concrete individuals, and not only because their names remained unknown. The point was rather that the Germans were a species, and distinguishing individual specimens would be pointless, given that all of them—

whether in the ghetto or on the Aryan Side—were doing the same things to Jews and existed for this one purpose. They were a species establishing a new order and ruthlessly carrying out its laws, a species of executioners calling themselves Germans. Individuations were superfluous; a mouse being hunted by a cat doesn't pause to reflect upon whether the cat is charcoal-colored or black. Whether the cat goes by Felix or another name is all the same to the mouse. I hear that in recent years a distinct tendency has emerged to call those who conceived of and carried out the Final Solution not Germans, but Nazis—and in this way not burden the whole nation with responsibility for the crime. At the time, though, people spoke only of Germans. Even today, I wouldn't know how to use a different word in this context, even though I'm aware, of course, that not every member of that nation became a hired assassin during those times, some might have not known what their fellow countrymen were doing—although here a thought comes to me that often does with respect to such situations: societies don't know what they don't want to know.

So in the years after the war ended did the phrase "Germans are people" seem to me to express a radical falsity, to ennoble those undeserving. For I understood that in this phrase "people" carried a particular normative value—even if I was not yet then struck by the extent to which this word was in some sense tinted with a certain polemicism. After all, the sentence implicitly comprises a response to something doubtful and ambiguous, for in no case would one claim that Frenchmen, Americans, or Poles were people—such obviousness isn't put into words. Still, is it possible to relate this word in its normative meaning—even acknowledging it as a response to generally harbored doubts—to those who created a world of iniquity, who killed so many people? (Here the word is used appropriately!) And do I, whom they also desired to murder (that this did not come about was due only to a whole series of fortuitous coincidences, if not miracles, together with the aid of wonderful people who often exposed themselves to death) have a right to apply this word to Germans?

Not long ago I became aware that in its ghetto- or occupation-era usage, the term "Germans" referred primarily, if not exclusively, to men. In principle, women did not come into play, surely not because they were judged more refined and believed not to have participated in the sordid enterprise. In those years I definitely hadn't heard of such concentration camp heroines as Ilse Koch; only after the war did I learn of female criminals, just as it was only many years later in documentary films that I saw flocks of young girls staging demonstrations in their leader's honor, and hysterical old ladies falling over themselves in ecstasy, worshipping their Führer. At the time I associated Germans exclusively with men; this is what experience taught, and most likely it never occurred to me that this name would encompass women as well. Undoubtedly women, too, contributed to what happened, although to a lesser degree and in a less spectacular way.

What elicited fear and became the embodiment of iniquity was a German, a German in uniform; I didn't then know about white-collar murderers who sat behind a desk, at least some of whom wore civilian clothing. I understood that to me, my family, the inhabitants of the ghetto, and later those hiding on the Aryan Side, a German could do anything he liked—that is, torture and kill. He could do so because he was master of life and death in the most literal sense, and this was true regardless of whether he vaunted the rank of general or was an ordinary private or even a downtrodden underling among his own people. And you, subject to his authority, were not even a serf—from the very outset you were done for, destined for the gallows, with the sentence in your case having already been handed down, and you could count on no mitigating circumstances, no possibility of reprieve, nothing that might save your life. Racial ideology precludes deviations, allows for no exceptions, and is ruthlessly deterministic. In those years, of course, I didn't think in such terms—I wouldn't have known how to articulate things this way—nonetheless my present formulation conveys the knowledge I possessed at the time, almost certainly a universal knowledge among those who fell subject to the Final Solution, regardless of their age. Germans were those who annihilated Jews consistently, programmatically, and mercilessly, and in essence existed in order to torment, torture, and kill, at first one by one or in fairly small groups, and later—when the era of transports arrived and the name of the little-known locality of Treblinka acquired a sinister tone—en masse. Gleaning an awareness of these truths required no special effort. This was commonplace knowledge in the most precise meaning of the word and required no instruction or initiation in its secrets, it arose from everyday experience.

I feared Germans and hated them. If someone had told me then that there were "good Germans," I wouldn't have believed it; at most they might be characters from some fantastical tale, dwelling beyond the borders of our real world, beyond the range of the imagination. I hadn't seen a "good German," I'd seen only killers. And a German who was not an executioner, or at least did not want to be, was nonetheless perceived as a murderer, this resulted from his role and social position. In the terror-laden world of the occupation there was no escape from the executioner, even if one managed to escape his mortal blows in a given instance. There was fear, the most piercing and extreme fear, because we knew life was at stake, and there was hatred, but there was also a feeling of helplessness and an awareness that no one had the ability to oppose the Germans—who after all were not people— or to avert what they were up to, in any case not here and now. For in those rare moments when a fleeting shadow of optimism flickered on the horizon, the adults would dream up scenarios of how things would be after the Germans were defeated. The thought that the criminal against whom one was wholly defenseless would be overcome must have brought solace, if only for a moment.

Nor were visions of this kind, experienced in forms accessible to a young child, foreign to me. One day in late July or early August 1942—and thus at a time when the *Aktion* of transports to Treblinka was in full operation—a violent storm passed over Warsaw. Or perhaps there was no storm and everything took place in the sphere of my hallucinations. Today it's no longer important. Evening approached, and I was lying in bed but not yet asleep, perhaps in that difficult-to-define space suspended somewhere between wakefulness and sleep. And suddenly I imagined raging lightning bolts, they left people and their homes untouched, they were directed only at the Germans. In front of my eyes I saw how the lightning bolts struck the Germans' buildings, destroying them, and above all killing the Germans themselves. I delighted in how their elegant, impeccably clean uniforms were transformed into *shmates* dripping with blood. These hallucinations passing through my consciousness gave me great, indeed sadistic, satisfaction. It fascinated me that the executioners were themselves victims, and that those powerful and handsome men came to resemble, if only as the result of the storm, those whom they humiliated, persecuted, and ultimately murdered. These visions from the border of sleep and wakefulness were remarkably concrete, and at the time I was ready to believe them. They did not fade when I realized they were only fantasies in which my wishes and dreams had found a voice. Nor did they fade when I recognized that the lightning bolts—real or imagined—had not struck where they ought to have, that the storm had passed, the world of the perishing ghetto surrounding me was entirely unaltered, and nothing had happened to any German as a result of the powerful discharges of electricity— which perhaps after all I had only dreamt. The lightning bolts had not reached even the worst of the worst. Many years later, I think that those fantasies at the border of sleep and wakefulness captured my imagination not because I believed, even if only for a moment, in a just order assured by nature or God, but because I was seeking consolation and I wished for this to happen. I wanted to believe that from somewhere deliverance would be forthcoming. It was not forthcoming in the real world, so I envisioned its being borne by thunderbolts from a convulsing sky. More than half a century later, I wonder whether those visions floating before my eyes that summer evening carried a hint of the fascination an executioner can hold for his victim.

I don't recall dreaming at any later point of nature's turning against the Germans and bringing succor to the persecuted. Perhaps I'd lost all hope, or perhaps, like the adults, I believed that only the defeat of the Germans would bring liberation. In any case, when I was hiding on the Aryan Side, I also knew that Germans were those who wanted to kill me, and when they caught me, they would realize this aim with complete certainty. Such was the fundamental definition of a German; in this respect nothing either had or could have changed. I knew that I could fall into German hands only once, just like a minesweeper commits an error only once.

Later in my childhood, in the period just after the war, Germans symbolized—or personified—all that was evil. I knew what they had done, what kind of world they had created, how many awful crimes they had committed, and how many people they had killed—among them, people I knew and remembered, like my closest cousin, Adaś Rozenowicz, younger than me by just a few months. It was not that I thought of this constantly, that I constantly returned to the terrible memories; this image of Germans cast by the experience of the Holocaust existed in my consciousness as something fully formed and self-evident from the outset, not even requiring verbalization, just as all things and observations not subject to doubt require no particular articulation. For precisely this reason, I reacted with such sharp astonishment to the sentence "Germans are people." It evoked in me not only distaste, but also repugnance, and to this day I remember it.

I have not drawn up an account of injuries; this would be superfluous, since the general tally has become universally known. Cruel visions like those that came into my head one summer evening during the ghetto's liquidation no longer thrust themselves upon me, and images of justice being delivered to the Germans—by the force of nature or God, the victors, or whomever or whatever else—ceased to entice me. I didn't think about revenge, perhaps because I realized that what had been done could not be rejoined by anything like it, if one did not want to apply the principle "an eye for an eye," which in contemporary reality would mean "a gas chamber for a gas chamber." I'm not certain whether I reflected upon that then—most likely not, although I must have heard some opinions on the topic—yet here I'm not writing of reasoned views, I'm endeavoring rather to reconstruct my feelings, to reconstruct what filled my consciousness, the consciousness of a teenage boy who had, by an utter miracle, slipped away from death and seen the world he lived in murdered.

May I speak here of hatred? I don't think it was the word most apt at that moment, although it did occupy some place within the gamut of emotions that shaped my attitude toward Germans. I would point above all to contempt and revulsion. Contempt for those who perpetrated the most sordid crimes and who were not people; revulsion toward those who were capable of doing what no one else had done, of acts transcending all that had been imaginable. The contempt and revulsion coexisted harmoniously with each other and were yoked not with the thought of revenge, but rather with something else, something difficult to define precisely and unambiguously. I'm not finding the right expression and so will put the matter in these words: I hold Germans in such contempt, I'm so repulsed by them, that I never again want to have anything to do with them. I never in my life want to cross paths with them, and thus I must act as if they have ceased to exist. I don't ever want to find myself near a German again, I don't want to brush past him or touch him, just as I wouldn't want to touch shit. Contempt and revulsion possess a concrete, even corporeal, dimension: the consequence of this is the idea of complete isolation. One has no desire to enter into alliances with murderers, nor to converse with them or have any kind of contact with them.

This was how I saw Germans in the period immediately following the war, when I was an adolescent. My perception of Germans had an integral character. No doubts crept in, and in principle nothing disturbed it. In my real world there was no longer anyone whom I could define by the word "German." Germans belonged to the most terrible of pasts, but still the past. At the time I took no interest in politics, I paid no attention to the

Germans' fate after their defeat; only the most important events reached me, the ones I couldn't fail to hear about. Nor was I overly moved by these events, I wanted to forget about the Germans' existence, just as one desires to plunge nightmares into oblivion. I wanted to forget them, or at least suppress my memories of them in such a way that they would return as seldom as possible. I never fully succeeded.

My attitude toward Germans encompassed people; matters became more complicated with respect to German culture. After a radio appeared in our home after the war, I became fascinated with music—though not with the dance music or show tunes that dominated the radio programs. I loved Bach, passionately and uncritically, upon my first hearing. I quickly came to regard him as the greatest composer ever to have appeared in the world (a youthful view to which I remain faithful). I followed the programs published in the newspaper so as not to miss any piece by Bach played on Polish radio. I didn't think about his being a German. For me, Bach was Bach, just as Mozart was Mozart, Beethoven was Beethoven, and Brahms was Brahms. German music per se ceased to exist—and not only for me, this was, I think, a wider phenomenon. After all, and notwithstanding the prohibitions, those great classical composers were also played in the ghetto, and Polish musicians performed their works in the cafés of occupied Warsaw. During my youthful fascination with music, I would have been astounded had someone told me that these ingenious composers represented German culture. Bracketing this fact, casting it beyond the threshold of consciousness, became a precondition to listening to their works. Facilitating this, moreover, was the fact that, at least with respect to Bach, it was mainly his instrumental compositions that were played (in Poland during the first postwar decade vocal pieces written to German texts were generally performed in translation). It was simply music. There was also German music, generally not recalled at that time, represented by Wagner, whom the Nazis— that is, the Germans—had treated as their patron. His work could not simply belong to music. And although my musical tastes are broad and not confined to specific epochs or types, I was never interested in Wagner; I never grew to like him, and not only for the reason that I lack a taste for endlessly grandiloquent operas. The emotions and prejudices of my youth never dissipated. It was somewhat more difficult to establish that German literature was not German literature. I don't remember when I first read a book by a German author, I can't recall what it might have been. With curiosity I devoured Hans Fallada's novel *Every Man Dies for Himself,* famous in its time. While it was undoubtedly difficult for me to penetrate that alien German world, I was interested in how it appeared from the inside. At university I was made to read several German classics; familiarity with them was obligatory for the examination in world literature. I approached reading Goethe and Schiller without resistance; I didn't reflect upon it, I must have regarded them as part of European culture. My first encounter with the work of Thomas Mann was a tremendous experience for me. A small collection of stories fell into my hands, among them *Tonio Kröger,* which at once became my favorite novella. In that case, reading this contemporary German author did not necessitate accepting further assumptions or overcoming distaste; I knew that Mann had been an opponent of the Nazis and had spent the entirety of the Nazi period in emigration. If "a good German" was at all conceivable, it was he. And after all, was he really a German writer? Perhaps he was simply a writer, just as Johann Sebastian Bach was simply a composer, in both cases, without the national qualifier.

As I speak of how someone like myself—who survived the Warsaw Ghetto and hiding on the Aryan Side, and had constantly in his memory the notion that a German was a beast who would immediately kill you were you to fall into his hands— saw Germans and things German, I cannot but ask about one thing: did the anti-German propaganda flourishing after 1945 have an influence on my attitude and perspective? The propaganda was meant to serve various functions, among them the legitimation of the new communist authorities, yet it seems to me that in cases such as mine, it was entirely superfluous. My view of Germans was so unambiguous and so axiomatically uniform that it would have been difficult to intensify it in any way. As did almost everyone, I succumbed in various realms to the unearthly cannonade of propaganda reverberating with varying intensity from the first days of People's Poland; in this sphere, though, I preserved a sobriety of intellect, all the more so as anti-German propaganda was becoming part of anti-Western propaganda or, rather, most often a pretext for the latter. They spoke of Germans, but meant America, and to me this was no longer persuasive.

From the time an entity by the name of the German Democratic Republic appeared on the map, that propaganda began to feel to me manifestly false or simply absurd—something for which I credit myself, given that people incomparably more mature than I, even great female writers otherwise ill-disposed toward communism, succumbed to it. It was truly difficult for me to believe that on one side of the border lived only evil Germans, while on the other there lived only good ones, and that I should accordingly hate the former but love the latter. When this style of propaganda became dominant I was first in school and later beginning university; I was uninitiated in its mysteries and unable to understand its mechanisms, yet in this matter I harbored no doubts—it was pure nonsense. I considered apologias for the GDR, repeated brazenly for several decades, to be something inordinately deceitful and out of place. The dichotomies were so primitively constructed that it was impossible not to discard them, which for me brought about no difficulties, because in truth it was all the same to me on which side of the Elbe Germans resided. Germans on both sides were equally alien to me, and I wanted nothing to do with either. I thought the worst about both, always in connection with what had happened during the black seasons. As a rule, in reading the press I skipped anything that had to do with Germans. Yet at a certain moment, many years after the war, I came to understand that it was not possible to ignore their existence in Europe. This I treated as a political problem, by nature distant from me, given that I'm not nor will I ever be a politician. I received the famous bishops' letter of

1965 with understanding—and not even because the idea of forgiveness appealed to me (I had never contemplated this), but rather because I apprehended that the constant stoking of hostility toward Germans strengthened Poland's dependence on Russia. I took that letter as an important gesture, though it failed to influence my attitude toward Germans. They continued to make up a world that was utterly alien, and it continued to be difficult for me to believe that "people are there, souls they bear."

Before 1963 I had no personal encounters with Germans nor did I wish for such interaction, I lived in a sealed country—although sealed less hermetically after 1956 than during the years of high Stalinism—so there was no occasion for it. I don't know how I would have reacted in the first years after the war had I encountered a German—most likely I wouldn't have wanted to speak to him at all. In 1963 I spent eight months in Paris. The institution overseeing foreign students on scholarships would organize weekend trips to various historical sites and places of interest, and I took part readily, the fees were not exorbitant, and I wanted to see as much as possible, I felt as if I had been released from a cage and didn't know when—if ever—I would again escape abroad. In the course of these trips I interacted with people from different countries, even from different parts of the world, as there were many Latin Americans. I spoke with them in French, yet soon I noticed that some of those with whom I spoke French spoke German among themselves. They had appeared to me to be kind, open, and intelligent, but when I heard their native language, I was grieved and discomfited. It was simply difficult for me to reconcile myself to the fact that I was engaging in admittedly rather conventional yet nonetheless amiable interactions with Germans. I didn't make this apparent, but I did feel ill at ease. I regarded what I was doing as deeply improper, something that in its own way constituted an act of disloyalty to the whole of my previous life, and above all an act of betrayal toward those—family as well as strangers—who had perished. At a certain moment, I tried to regain my sense of well-being with the thought that these were German-speaking Swiss, or in a worse case, Austrians (despite everything, Austrians seemed less horrible to me than Germans, perhaps because people prefer not to think about the fact that their participation in crimes was quite substantial). When I had better oriented myself in the situation, I was forced to part with my illusions. These were Germans. This caused me to think.

I began to ponder whether I could have the same relationship to these young people, my contemporaries or (most often) a bit younger, as I did to all other Germans. I was not yet familiar with the expression applied to this generation, "the grace of a late birth," by, if I'm not mistaken, Chancellor Kohl. At the time, this phrase had not yet come into being, but it does give expression to a certain fact which it was impossible not to notice: at the time of Hitler's reign these people had been too young to participate in the great mechanism of iniquity, even in an auxiliary role. Of course I might have accepted the premise that the crimes of the father are passed to the son, that transgressions so terrible they cannot be cleansed effect a collective responsibility, and that the sin of genocide implicates everyone who did, does, or will belong to the society of murderers. Such a conception must have seemed to me at once too simplistic and too irrational to be satisfying. Thus out of necessity I was forced to acknowledge that a new element should be introduced into my relationship to Germans—the generational factor. My desire is to think rationally, so I cannot blame those who lived outside the Nazi state's sphere of influence during the black seasons, nor can I direct my resentment to those who were children at the time or not yet born. The generational criterion became a lasting component of my perception of Germans and has retained its influence to this day, even though more than half a century has passed since the end of the war.

There was nothing profound in my interaction with those with whom I visited Rouen or the castles on the Loire; these were brief and casual encounters with people who remained anonymous to me. I came into closer contact with a young German a year later, in Warsaw. He spoke Polish with an obvious accent, but well, and there were no problems in communicating. He had come to improve his knowledge of the language, but above all to collect material for a study of Mickiewicz. Presently he is an eminent professor of Slavic studies, an outstanding expert on—and seasoned translator of—Polish literature from Kochanowski to Gombrowicz; I could converse with him on various subjects, and without reservation treat him as a colleague. Only once was I repulsed and sickened: on some occasion he confessed that in 1933 his father had actively supported Hitler and had belonged to one of the Nazi organizations or even a fighting squad. I told this to my excellent friend Zofia Stefanowska, who asked me, "Do you think that good Germans were brought by storks?" I conceded that those lovely birds had played no role here, just as years later I had to concur that neither had storks brought good Russians. This thought came to my mind when I grew aware that numerous dissidents, bravely fighting the monster of totalitarianism, were the sons—or more often the grandsons—of Stalinist dignitaries who bore terrifying things on their conscience.

Afterward every so often I would come across Germans from both halves of the divided country. I even knew well one who, having grown bored of the GDR, resolved to Polonize himself, an endeavor in which he succeeded. No longer did such contacts elicit deeper emotions in me, all the more so as these were most often casual contacts, confined to professional matters, all with Germans availing themselves of the privilege of a late birth. I had the most such encounters in 1973 to 1974 when I spent a year at the university in Amsterdam. It was precisely then that I became fully aware of how I still treated Germans in a way unlike the way I treated everyone else, of how I was still unable to avoid thinking about what had happened during the black seasons and unable to forget what I'd experienced. I still see in Germans people who are tainted, people who will never be able to rid themselves of their great sin. Two minor incidents testified to this.

I thought of my yearlong stay in Holland as an opportunity

to use university breaks for travel around Europe. This meant
long waits in consulates and scrambles for visas. As a rule I didn't
encounter problems, the exception being the German consulate.
The same office clerk always dealt with me, she was a formidable
blond no longer in her youth, odiously unpleasant, who treated
me as if I were her personal enemy. She clearly wanted to make
difficulties for me, and when I showed her my invitation from
the university in Bochum—I had then, for the first time in my
life, resolved to go to Germany—she questioned its authenticity. I don't want to relate more about her, as it's my reaction that
interests me. Had this been an office clerk of any other national-
ity, I most likely would have thought: what a repugnant, mean-
spirited beldame, and perhaps—interior monologues being often more vulgar than those voiced aloud—the beautiful term
"bureaubitch" would have come to mind. And doubtlessly it
would have ended with that. But things proceeded differently
with this stalwart blond, who looked as if she had been a spe-
cially bred, indeed exemplary, specimen of the Nordic race, according to the Nazi imagination. In her I saw a German, and thus
an embodiment of a species and a symbol of a nation. And at once
I imagined her decades earlier, during her now distant youth,
marching in a procession with the appropriate banners, shouting out slogans in honor of Hitler. There was even more: I saw
her as a guard in a concentration camp, a beast from Auschwitz
or Ravensbrück. The path from executioner to malevolent con-
sular clerk revealed itself to be as straightforward as it was short.
This was not because I was upset or overcome by emotions and
so unable to think calmly and objectively, my experiences simply
spoke up, as they always do when a relevant situation arises, such
as when I read about German skinheads persecuting foreigners
or profaning Jewish cemeteries. In such cases the line of conti-
nuity comes very distinctly into view.

I overcame the resistance of this hideous bureaucrat, and for
the first time in my life, I went to Germany for several days. One
of those days I decided to spend roaming about Cologne. And it

was just here that there came about the second incident, unto itself devoid of any significance. Had it been another place and another person, I would have immediately forgotten it. At a certain moment an older man approached me, he was looking for a street, and he asked me where it was. I don't know German, yet I managed to pull myself together enough to stammer that I didn't know because I was in Cologne for the first time. He smiled from ear to ear, slapped me amiably on the shoulder and said something along the lines of: and haven't I asked the right person! I shuddered, and not at all because I don't like being slapped. Instantaneously, with unusual rapidity and without any reflection, I thought: and what the hell were you, you son of a bitch, doing *then*?! Now you're being nice, but how can I be certain that in those times you weren't shooting at innocent people, leading people to the gas, taking part in executions? A minor event, in itself meaning nothing, caused me to feel especially alienated in that city—and not because I didn't know anyone there. When I crossed the border and found myself in Maastricht, I breathed deeply, feeling as if I had returned to a world where I needn't worry that ghosts of the past would peer out from behind every corner.

For many years afterward I was not in Germany. I only passed through it by train. Many times I thought of treating myself to a trip to Leipzig to see the city of Johann Sebastian Bach and especially the Thomaskirche, so strongly tied to his life and work. It was there that most of his cantatas were performed for the first time, cantatas which constitute the summits of music (or so I've felt since longer than I can remember). After a certain point, travel from the Polish People's Republic to the German Democratic Republic caused no particular problems, yet I could never bring myself to make such a trip. After the destruction of the wall I was twice in Germany, in Berlin and Erlangan, and I have good memories of both of those visits. The passing of time meant that I now interacted only with those who benefited from the grace of a late birth. This eased the situation, of course, even

though I did not forget for even a moment about all that happened half a century ago. No longer was I so troubled by the sentence from Mickiewicz's hero's monologue, although I continued to associate it with fundamental questions. ". . . Germans,
too, are people"—but are they really people like everyone else?
I remain unable to rid myself of doubts.

❁

Translator's Notes

Fragments from the Ghetto

5

at the very beginning of the war, right after the defeat

> This refers to Poland's defeat by Nazi Germany. On September 1, 1939, Nazi Germany attacked Poland. For weeks Poland resisted the invasion, before being forced to capitulate on September 28.

7

watching Andrzej Wajda's black-and-white film about Janusz Korczak

> Janusz Korczak (1878–1942), a Polish Jew, was a famous doctor, author, and educator in interwar Poland. In 1940, the orphanage he ran for Jewish children became part of the Warsaw Ghetto. Korczak, together with the children from his orphanage, was deported from Umschlagplatz and died in the gas chambers of Treblinka.

11

just before the beginning of the *Aktion,* the transports to Treblinka

> In July 1942 the Nazis commenced the liquidation of the Warsaw Ghetto, beginning mass deportations of the ghetto's residents from Umschlagplatz to the gas chambers of Treblinka.

13

team of *szaulisi* and *czubaryki* assisting the Germans

> The reference is to Lithuanians and other ethnic minorities serving the Germans as auxiliary police.

15

we could see and hear the Aryan Side

> The "Aryan Side" was the term used to designate the area beyond the Warsaw Ghetto wall where Warsaw's non-Jewish inhabitants lived.

The Pastry

18

in the ghetto these children were called *hots-rakhmunes*

> The term comes from the Yiddish phrase *hots rakhmunes* meaning "have mercy!"

Emil

21

right by the wall, not visible (or imaginable) from the Aryan Side

> The original phrase translated here as "not visible (or imaginable) from the Aryan Side" reads "którego nie można było badać od marzeń strony" and is an allusion to the poem "Dziewczyna" by Bolesław Lesmian.

Beans and a Violin

37

perished in that terrible meaning of the word 'perish,' which
had become axiomatic at that time, perished together with the
young man

The original word translated here as "perish" is *zginąć.* See
the discussion of this term in the Translator's Preface.

Getting Out

39

the phrase "getting out"

The original word translated here as "getting out" is *wyjście.*
The Polish term is a verbal noun from the verb *wyjść,* meaning to leave, to exit, to get out. This verbal noun *wyjście* is
also used as the noun "exit" in Polish. It further appears in
the phrase *nie ma wyjścia* meaning "there is no exit," "there
is no other choice," "there is no way out." In this chapter the
author plays with different forms of the verb *wyjść,* teasing
out the range of the word's meanings.

41

szmalcownicy

Szmalcownicy was the term used to refer to Poles who, during
the Nazi occupation of Poland, extorted money from Jews
hiding on the Aryan Side by threatening to reveal their
whereabouts to the Gestapo.

42

a Jewish eye would better be able to assess 'bad looks'

The phrase "bad looks," or *zły wygląd* in the original Polish,
is a specific Polish expression referring to an outwardly
Semitic appearance that would make it difficult, if not
impossible, for a Jew to "pass" as a non-Jew. The expression

has a complement, *dobry wygląd,* meaning "good looks" and used in reference to a Jew whose physical features were not stereotypically Semitic and who therefore could "pass" as a Pole.

42

an unfamiliar man who, oddly enough, turned out to be a blue policeman

"Blue policeman" refers to a member of the *policja granatowa* (literally "blue police"), a police force composed of Poles operating in the General Government in collaboration with the Germans.

Długi

46

He was called Długi

Długi is a Polish adjective meaning "long."

47

His Polish was odd—he spoke the bad Polish typical of Jews—

"He spoke the bad Polish typical of Jews" is a translation of the Polish expression *żydłaczyć,* meaning to distort the Polish language in a way typical of a native Yiddish speaker.

49

just short of fifty hectares

Property over fifty hectares was subject to nationalization under the 1945 Communist law on agricultural reform.

51

Anschluss

Anschluss is the German word referring to Hitler's 1938 annexation of Austria to Nazi Germany.

51

allocating his property to a *Treuhänder,* a role filled by a *Volks-deutscher* from Poznan

> *Treuhänder* is a German word meaning "trustee"; *Volks-deutscher* refers to a person who is not a German citizen but is of ethnic German origin. Polish citizens in this category were given a higher status than ethnic Poles under the Nazi occupation of Poland.

53

as Mary Berg relates in her moving diary

> *Warsaw Ghetto: A Diary* by Mary Berg was published in English in 1945 after appearing in serial form in Yiddish the year before. Berg was fifteen years old when she began her diary in 1939, following the Nazi invasion of Poland. She and her family were imprisoned in the Warsaw Ghetto. That they managed to escape deportations was due to the fact that Mary Berg's mother possessed American citizenship. The family was eventually sent to an internment camp in France; after being exchanged for German prisoners, Berg's family went to the United States.

55

he was active in the Home Army

> The Home Army (*Armia Krajowa,* or AK) was a Polish underground resistance fighting against the Nazis. The AK subordinated itself to the Polish government-in-exile in London.

57

he would soon be classified as a *kulak,* a class enemy

> *Kulak* is a Russian word that literally means "fist," but is used to refer to a more prosperous (that is, less indigent) peasant. "Dekulakization," the Bolshevik campaign to purge the wealthier (in practice, less impoverished) peasants, was a central component of collectivization.

The Villa on Odolańska Street

75

in the area that was once the ghetto or in Mokotów

Mokotów refers to a district of Warsaw just south of the city center.

77

Irena Sendlerowa

Irena Sendlerowa, born in 1910, belonged to the underground organization Żegota, the Council for Aid to the Jews, which was connected to the Home Army and the Polish government-in-exile in London. She smuggled food, medicine, and money into the Warsaw Ghetto and arranged hiding places for Jewish children on the Aryan Side. In 2003 she was awarded the Jan Karski prize for her work in saving Jewish children during the Holocaust.

The House beneath the Eagles

84

in Zakopane style

"Zakopane style" refers to a style of wooden architecture reminiscent of Polish homes in the Tatra mountains, in particular in the mountain resort town of Zakopane and the surrounding area. Typical features included porches, stone foundations, steep and conical roofs, and windows finished in a semicircle. This architectural style was popularized at the end of the nineteenth century by the architect and painter Stanisław Witkiewicz (father of the painter and author Stanisław Ignacy Witkiewicz, known as Witkacy).

85

The Cross and the Mezuzah

Helena Szereszewska's memoirs, originally published in Polish as *Krzyż i mezuza,* appeared in an English translation by Anna Marianska in 1997 under the title *Memoirs from Occupied Warsaw, 1940–1945.*

88

A ceaseless *psychomachia* went on in that villa.

A Greek word meaning "a struggle or fight for life," "Psychomachia" is the title of a poem by Prudentius from c. 400 A.D. Prudentius used the term in the sense of an internal conflict, a battle between the spirit and the flesh.

A Quarter Hour Passed in a Pastry Shop

92

a couple living in Ochota

Ochota is a district of Warsaw just southwest of the city center.

95

in the possession of the Erinyes, the Furies

In Greek mythology the Erinyes, or Furies, were underworld deities who extracted vengeance against those who committed specific crimes. They were winged creatures with serpents for hair who punished violations against the natural order of things. They appear perhaps most famously in Aeschylus's *Oresteia.*

Jasio the Redhead

98

from Lwów

Lwów/Lviv/Lvov/Lemberg is a city in eastern Galicia. It was
part of the Hapsburg Empire before World War I, and sub-
sequently a part of interwar Poland. Following the Soviet
invasion of Poland in September 1939, Polish Lwów became
the Soviet Ukrainian city of Lvov (Russian) or Lviv (Ukrainian); it is today the Ukrainian city of Lviv.

100

the way people spoke in Lwów and the eastern borderlands

The eastern borderlands, *kresy* in Polish, refers to the eastern
part of what was interwar Poland, an area inhabited largely
by Ukrainian, Belarusian, and Jewish ethnic minorities.

The Death of Sister Longina

104

a figure associated with the January Uprising

The January Uprising, begun in January 1863, was an unsuccessful attempt to liberate the lands of the former Polish–
Lithuanian Commonwealth from the Russian Empire.

A Louse on a Beret, a Chasuble, a Pair of Shoes

135

with the intention of settling in the Recovered Territories

The so-called Recovered Territories, *Ziemie odzyskane,* refers
to lands that belonged to Germany in the interwar years and
were assigned to Poland (in compensation for the loss of the
eastern territories to the Soviet Union) after World War II.

135

I remember that ride through beautiful surroundings. The road led through forest hillocks, through no longer green meadows, lightly yellowed but still magnificent, fields that enticed the eyes with their many colors.

The author here uses the phrase "droga bowiem wiodła wśród pagórków leśnych, łąk może już nie zielonych," an allusion to the epic poem *Pan Tadeusz,* in which the Romantic poet Adam Mickiewicz (1798–1855) writes, "Do tych pagórków leśnych, do tych łąk zielonych" (into those forest hillocks, into those green meadows).

136

We arrived in the Praga district

The Praga district is that district of Warsaw lying on the east side of the Vistula River.

Misjudeja

144

a soldier in Berling's Army

In 1943, following the break in diplomatic relations between the Soviet Union and the Polish government-in-exile, Stalin gave his permission for a Polish army division to be created in the Soviet Union with the purpose of fighting alongside the Red Army. The Polish division was led by General Zygmunt Berling.

It Was I Who Killed Jesus

152

which in accordance with custom was still named after
Piłsudski

> Following a military coup in May 1926, Marshal Józef Pił-
> sudski became the effective dictator of interwar Poland and
> remained so until his death in 1935.

152

don't know if he especially liked Lolitas

> The reference here is to the novel *Lolita,* by Vladimir
> Nabokov.

153

a certain Beilis

> In 1911, Menachem "Mendel" Beilis, a Jewish factory man-
> ager, was arrested by tsarist police in Kiev on accusations of
> the ritual murder of a Christian boy, whom Beilis had al-
> legedly killed in order to use the boy's blood as an ingredi-
> ent in Passover matzo. Beilis was acquitted in a jury trial in
> 1913, but not before the case had attracted international
> attention.

157

a certain article by Father Tischner

> Józef Tischner (1931–2000) was a Polish priest and eminent
> philosopher, founder of the Cracovian Papal Academy of The-
> ology and cofounder of the Institut für die Wissenschaften
> vom Menschen in Vienna. The author of many books and
> articles and Solidarity's chaplain, Father Tischner enjoyed
> enormous moral authority both in Poland and abroad.

Books I Didn't Read in My Youth

160

lokomotywa Tuwima

> "Lokomotywa" ("The Locomotive") is among the most famous children's poems by the luminary Polish poet Julian Tuwim (1894–1953).

164

He read *The Trilogy*

> *The Trilogy* consists of three historical novels by the Polish author Henryk Sienkiewicz (1846–1916) set in the mid-seventeenth century: *Ogniem i mieczem* (*With Fire and Sword,* 1884), *Potop* (*The Deluge,* 1886) and *Pan Wolodyjowski* (*Colonel Wolodyjowski,* 1888).

Germans Are People, Too

169

a play by Leon Kruczkowski

> Leon Kruczkowski (1900–62) began his professional life as a chemist before becoming a writer. A reserve officer of the Polish Army, he was called to active duty in September 1939 and soon captured by the Germans; he spent over five years as a prisoner-of-war. Upon returning to Poland, he became a leading figure in the cultural realm during the Stalinist years.

169

a modernized citation from *Konrad Wallenrod*

> The epic poem *Konrad Wallenrod* was written by the Polish Romantic poet Adam Mickiewicz.

171

after seeing at Zachęta an exhibit of photographs

Zachęta is an art gallery located in the center of Warsaw.

173

such concentration camp heroines as Ilse Koch

The wife of Karl Koch, commandant of the Nazi concentration camp Buchenwald, Ilse Koch was herself a guard and later overseer at the camp. She was known as "Die Hexe von Buchenwald" (the witch from Buchenwald) and "The Bitch of Buchenwald" for her particularly cruel and sadistic behavior. After the war, she was tried and found guilty by a war crimes tribunal and later by a German court. She hanged herself at Aibach prison in 1967.

180

from the first days of People's Poland

People's Poland refers to Poland under Communist rule.

180–81

famous bishops' letter of 1965

In November 1965, Polish bishops sent a Letter of Reconciliation to German bishops in which they wrote, "we forgive and ask forgiveness."

181

"people are there, souls they bear"

In the original: "tam są ludzie i tam mają dusze." The reference is to a work by the Polish poet Juliusz Slowacki (1809–49) entitled "Hymn (Bogarodzico!)" (Hymn [Mother of God!]).

About the Author

Michał Głowiński is among the most renowned literary scholars in Poland and the author of numerous works of literary criticism, history, and theory. He is a longtime professor at the Institute of Literary Studies at the Polish Academy of Sciences in Warsaw.

❧

Jewish Lives

For a complete list of titles, see the Northwestern University Press Web site at
www.nupress.northwestern.edu.